MIES VAN DER R

D1284468

BY PETER BLAKE

PELICAN BOOK A606

MIES VAN DER ROHE

ARCHITECTURE AND STRUCTURE

BY PETER BLAKE

PENGUIN BOOKS

Penguin Books Inc., 3300 Clipper Mill Road, Baltimore, Maryland

The Master Builders was originally published by Alfred A. Knopf Inc. This Pelican edition, taken from *The Master Builders,* first published 1964 by arrangement with Alfred A. Knopf Inc.

Reprinted 1966, 1968

Printed in the United States of America

FOR CHRISTINA, CASEY, KATHY, BILLY, AND ELIZABETH

ACKNOWLEDGEMENTS

I am particularly indebted to two people: first, to Mies van der Rohe himself, whom I have known for more than fifteen years, and whose fascinating reminiscences I have enjoyed throughout those same years. Needless to say, Mies never saw any part of this book until after it was published, and he is in no way responsible for any judgements of his own work – or of that of others – contained in this text. My second important source of information and, I suppose, of inspiration, was Philip C. Johnson, a long-time friend. Mr Johnson was, of course, the first biographer of Mies van der Rohe, and his crisp text on the architect's work, which was published by the Museum of Modern Art in 1947, remains the most authoritative record of Mies's early career.

It is characteristic of Mies that he himself has published almost nothing, and that he has encouraged very few others to publish his work. Indeed, references to Mies's early endeavours are scattered through dozens of 'little magazines' of the early 1920s; all of these magazines deserve credit for having recognized Mies's genius even when it was manifested only in projects and other sketchy proposals.

I should also like to thank Walter McQuade, Henry Robbins, and Ivan Von Auw for reading this manuscript and for offering many valuable suggestions. And I am grateful, too, for several weeks spent in splendid isolation at the College of Architecture at Cornell University (a place located somewhere near the North Pole); my time there enabled me to finish the more difficult parts of this book in peace.

PETER BLAKE
New York, 1963

This is the second volume in a series of monographs on three masters of modern architecture. The first dealt with the life and work of the French architect, Le Corbusier; the present volume deals with the German-born American, Ludwig Mies van der Rohe; and the third is concerned with the American architect, Frank Lloyd Wright.

Mies (as he is generally referred to) is a strange sort of artist to find in the twentieth century. Although his aesthetic theories and his completed buildings reveal a preoccupation with industrial technology, they also display an overriding concern with quality and perfection of detail, a concern which Mies shares with great craftsmen of the Renaissance, like Ghiberti, rather than with his contemporaries. The philosopher Hannah Arendt has written that 'in our need for more and more rapid replacement of the worldly things around us, we can no longer afford to . . . respect and preserve their inherent durability'. Yet, in trying to develop an architecture for an industrial age, Mies seems to have ignored this most obvious characteristic of our time, and made respect for quality and durability the primary criterion of his work.

This is, of course, in the best tradition of all art. As Miss Arendt says elsewhere, the 'durability [of works of art] is almost untouched by the corroding effect of natural processes . . . nowhere else does the sheer durability of the world of things appear in such purity and clarity'. In an age of throw-away furniture, throw-away cars, and throw-away houses, Mies has set himself the task of re-establishing fundamental values in architecture.

What are those fundamental values? Certainly they include qualities of space and of form, of proportion and of detail. It is true that the nature of space – or rather, the manner in which we see space today – has changed. It is true, also, that the forms we are able to create in our time are very different from those created in the past, for the 'bones' and the 'skin' which make those forms have changed radically.

9

But the essence of architecture remains much the same, and nowhere is this more apparent than in the work of Mies van der Rohe. The nobility of his spaces and the purity of his forms are more reminiscent of Palladio than they are of Sullivan; and his preoccupation with refinement and polish of detail is more intense than that of any of his contemporaries.

Is such a preoccupation merely pedantic and pointless in a mass-civilization? I think not. The most extraordinary quality of Mies's work is its apparent timelessness. Where the early buildings of Wright, Le Corbusier, Gropius, and others seem quite charmingly dated today, Mies's first structures are as modern now as they were when built forty years ago. Indeed, the best modern furniture, to this day, are the chairs, tables, benches, and stools designed by Mies more than thirty years ago – and they will probably look just as modern thirty years hence. If they were not so expensive, no modern architect would ever think of using any others.

What makes Mies's work timeless is his rejection of passing fads and dogmas, and his concentration upon pure form and pure detail. It is true that these objects which he has created – from stools to sky-scrapers – only *look* as if they had been industrially manufactured and are, in reality, the product of the most painstaking handicraft. But they are not handicrafted in spirit; in a sense they are conceived as prototypes for an industrial civilization, just as a beautifully hand-made automobile body by Pinin-Farina is a prototype for Detroit mass-production. What Mies has done – and no one else has done this in our time to quite the same degree – is to establish certain standards of excellence for industry to match. Unlike most modern architects, who seem both intrigued and intimidated by the resources of modern industry, Mies considers his mission to be one of leadership; it is the architect's job, in his view, to set an example to modern industry, to point the way towards quality in an age too much pre-occupied with quantity.

Unlike Frank Lloyd Wright, Mies van der Rohe has never resented imitation. Instead, he has welcomed it. 'Sometimes people say "How do you feel when somebody copies you?"' he told an interviewer not long ago. 'I say that is not a problem to me. I think that is the reason we are working, to find something that everybody can use.' He has seen his mission to be the creator of universal solutions, the setter of the highest possible standards, the avant-gardist who cares most profoundly about his followers. After all, there is only so much that one man can build in a lifetime; if he cares only about leaving monuments to himself, he will be satisfied with whatever he has built. But if he cares about the future of mankind, then he looks upon his own small output simply as a series of guideposts, each clear and convincing enough to point the way to future generations.

When the so-called 'International Style' produced its first buildings, many of these early products were formalist in the extreme: they were shapes and patterns inspired by Cubist painting and sculpture – yet, in reality, no more 'modern' than the stucco villas built along the shores of the Mediterranean for centuries past. Mies, like all others of his generation, was fond of these stucco cubes; but to him the essence of architecture has always been its content. That content had to be reasonable as well as beautiful; and in an age of enormously accelerated need for shelter, any architecture that did not resolve the problems of industrialized building was mere formalism. Mies's critics have said that he does not always follow the dictates of the industrial process. This is quite true. His mission has been to *direct* the industrial process. And that, precisely, is what gives his work its unique importance.

1. Mies van der Rohe in Chicago. (*Photo: Morley Baer*)

On almost any day of the week, around lunchtime, a massive man will climb up the delicate white steel and travertine staircase of the Chicago Arts Club. Although he now walks with a limp (due to recurring attacks of arthritis) and, generally, has to lean on a cane, Ludwig Mies van der Rohe seems remarkably nimble for his weight and age. His clothes are extremely elegant; most of his suits were tailored by Knize and make him look slim and agile. He is, indeed, something of a dandy in a subdued way: there is generally a very soft, very expensive handkerchief trailing out of his breast pocket, and he obviously likes fine quality in all his personal belongings.

Yet there is nothing dandified about his features: his head looks as if it has been chiselled out of a block of granite; his face, infinitely lined, has the massively aristocratic look of a wealthy Dutch burgher by Rembrandt. As he walks across the generous space of the Arts Club, which he designed in 1951, Mies – as everyone has learned to call him – may notice an acquaintance or greet a friend. When he does, his shy face suddenly lights up in a charming, rather toothy grin, and he may even say a word or two in a deep, hesitant voice. Later, after a couple of Martinis and lunch, Mies will pull out one of his huge cigars, relax, and even talk. It will then be about 2 p.m. Chicago time, and Mies will be ready to start on a new day in earnest.

No one seeing this large and impressive figure would suspect that Ludwig Mies (he added his mother's family name, van der Rohe, to his own when he started to work as an architect) was born the son of a rather humble mason and stone cutter. Nor would anyone suspect that this conservative gentleman, whose appearance is that of a Chairman of the Board of U.S. Steel or of some comparable Captain of Industry, has been considered a dangerous radical throughout a large part of his life. Indeed, as late as 1953, when Mies was already beginning to look a little bit like his own monument in rock, the editor of a woman's magazine hysterically attacked him as a 'threat to America' and hinted, darkly, that Mies was in league with Communists,

Fascists, and other nihilists. All of this came as a surprise not only to Mies himself, who is without question the gentlest radical ever to have renounced a barricade, but also to his friends, who have tried for years to protect him from the day-to-day tensions and conflicts of a neurotic era. The relative isolation in which he has lived has enabled him to concentrate, in peace and quiet, upon the search for simple truths which has been the central mission of his life as an architect.

Mies has not always been able to live so dedicated a life. He was born on 27 March 1886 in Aachen in the German Rhineland. His family's circumstances did not permit him to obtain any but the most rudimentary schooling. But the fact that his father was a master mason gave Mies a knowledge of building materials which many, more formally trained architects have never been able to acquire. 'My father had many wonderful blocks of marble and other stones in his shop,' Mies recalls, indicating with his hands a block of marble about a cubic foot in size. 'I learned about stone from him.' While attending elementary and trade schools, Mies earned a few pennies by working as a runner on construction projects, together with other boys of his age. 'We had to go out and get boiling hot water for the carpenters framing in the roof,' Mies recalls. 'They used the water to make coffee. And if we didn't get the water fast enough, they would throw one of their sharp axes after us to make us hurry up.' Mies is rather pleased with himself for having gone through this rough and tumble schooling, for having learned building not from the drawing board, but from the dirt and noise of the building site. When he is at ease – generally late in the evening, with a group of friends – he likes to talk about the days when he learned to put brick on brick. 'Now, a brick, that's really *some*thing,' he will say, with his infectious smile. 'That's really *building*. Not paper architecture.' There is some doubt as to how many bricks Mies ever really laid one on top of the other, for his father was a *stone* mason; but there is no doubt that he learned much of what there was to be known about building, in the traditional way, long before he drew a single line on paper. More than fifty years after he was born in the one-time seat of the Holy Roman Emperors, Mies made one of his rare, brief, and – to him – painful speeches at his inauguration as Director of Architecture at the Illinois Institute of Technology. On that day, in 1938, he said:

All education must begin with the practical side of life ... [along] the road of discipline from materials, through function, to creative work ... How sensible is the small, handy shape [of a brick], so useful for every

14

purpose! What logic in its bonding, pattern and texture! What richness in the simplest wall surface! But what discipline this material imposes! ...

'Discipline' – this has been the watchword of Mies's life and work. Discipline, order, clarity, truth. Aachen, the city of his birth, is located near the border between the Catholic Rhineland and the Low Countries, and Mies was born a Roman Catholic. Although he was never a practising member of his faith, the code to which he subscribed from his youth to this day – the code to which he added his own beliefs – is the moral code of St Augustine and of St Thomas Aquinas. He told that audience at Illinois Tech, in 1938: 'Nothing can express the aim and meaning of our work better than the profound words of St Augustine – "Beauty is the splendour of Truth."' To Mies, there has never been any doubt about the rightness, the truth – and hence the beauty – of what he was trying to do. Every step along his way has been a clear step – sure, steady, uncomplicated, uncompromising. The first step is the brick, the simple fact of the material. The second step is to understand the meaning of one material, and the meaning of all materials. The third step is to understand the materials characteristic of our time – steel, concrete, and glass. The fourth step is to understand the needs of our epoch: the need to provide vast amounts of shelter (the mass need); and the need to make each man free (the individual, human need). And the inevitable result of this clear and uncompromising progression is to ensure 'the splendour of truth'. How could it be otherwise? 'Our practical aims measure only our material progress,' Mies said. 'The values we profess reveal the level of our culture ... We must make clear, step by step, what things are possible, necessary and significant.' Mies's critics have sometimes tried to provoke him into arguments, to get him to defend his point of view. Mies considers such debates a waste of time; to him, logic – uncompromising logic – leads to truth, and truth leads to beauty. There is really nothing to discuss.

After leaving elementary school, Mies entered a local trade school, always concentrating on the practical aspects of building, always working, part time, on various buildings his father or his father's friends were putting up. When he was only fifteen years old, Mies left the trade school and apprenticed himself to several architects around Aachen. One of his major assignments of that period – a job he recalls with considerable amusement and some pride – was to make full-size drawings for neo-classical ornaments to be rendered in stucco on the façades of various buildings. 'We had to draw those things on huge sheets of paper pinned on a wall,' Mies recalled not long ago. 'No drawing-boards for us: we had to stand up, and draw this stuff swinging our arms in a big arc, covering the entire sheet with volutes and other decorative nonsense. That was real training in draughtsmanship!' It was also about as tough a job, physically, as splitting rocks on a chain gang, and Mies was delighted when, after two years of this particular kind of torture, he was offered a job by a Berlin architect. He left Aachen for the German capital in 1905. He was quite 'uneducated' in the conventional sense of the term. But, at an age when most young, would-be architects were just starting out at some academy, Mies knew much of what there was to be known about building, much of what there was to be known about self-discipline. At only nineteen he had acquired more valid knowledge than many architects acquire after years of academic training and apprenticeship.

Mies did not stay on his first Berlin job for very long. Upon discovering that his new employer worked primarily in wood, and upon realizing, furthermore, that he himself knew very little about that material, Mies went to Bruno Paul, the leading furniture designer of the period (who, like everyone else, was strongly influenced by Art Nouveau), and asked to become Paul's apprentice. After two years of apprenticeship, Mies had filled this particular gap in his working knowledge of building, and he left Paul's office. That year, 1907, Mies obtained his first commission, a house for a Professor Riehl in Neubabelsberg, a suburb of Berlin. Although the finished building was quite traditional in concept and detail, its perfect execution seemed almost incredible in a first work by a twenty-one-year-old apprentice.

There was one man working in Germany during the first decade of the twentieth century who appeared to have gone beyond the concept of the architect as an apostle of Arts and Crafts and a defender of man against the onslaught of the machine. That architect was Peter Behrens – the same Behrens to whom Le Corbusier was drawn in 1910, and who had employed the young Walter Gropius as one of his chief designers. When Mies finished his house for Professor Riehl, Behrens offered him a job in his office, and Mies accepted with delight; for three years Mies remained with Behrens and there, in effect, completed his architectural education.

Oddly enough, Behrens was important to Mies in two seemingly opposed ways: first, Mies learned from Behrens something of that potential interplay of architecture and industry which impressed Gropius and Le Corbusier so much during their periods in Behrens's office. But this was only a part of Behrens's work, however important; for, in addition to his industrial structures for the A.E.G. (the German electrical industry), and in addition to his 'product designs' for that same company, Behrens was occupied with another sort of practice which, to some of his admirers, seemed at violent odds with the 'advanced' work done for A.E.G. This other side of Behrens was his monumental, neo-classical work, generally for government agencies. And that work affected Mies almost as much as the 'new spirit' of industrialized building that was exemplified by Behrens's factories and exhibition structures.

This is not to suggest that Mies was really taken in by neo-classicism – or, for that matter, that Behrens was taken in. Around 1900 Behrens had been a leading apostle of Art Nouveau; he had designed some extraordinary plant-shaped glassware; he had done woodcuts almost indistinguishable, to a layman, from those being imported from Japan; and he had painted some delightfully sentimental canvases entitled *Mourning*, *The Kiss*, *Butterflies*, etc., that would have done credit to the most lachrymose pre-Raphaelite. By 1905, or thereabouts, the basic fallacy of Art Nouveau became shockingly apparent to Behrens, and he was looking for the cleansing influence of a clear and logical discipline – a classical discipline, to be precise – to help him pull out of the sentimental morass of Art Nouveau. He found that discipline in the neo-classicism of the great German architect of the early nineteenth century, Karl Friedrich Schinkel.

To Behrens, and to his young draughtsman, Mies, the most interesting aspects of Schinkel's neo-classicism were three: first, they felt that Schinkel had a way of placing his structures on wide pedestals or platforms that gave the buildings a considerable nobility; second, they saw that Schinkel had a feeling for rhythm, proportion, and scale which was applicable to buildings of *any* period; and, third, Behrens and Mies saw in Schinkel's buildings a purity of form which held even greater meaning for a time whose architectural forms and spaces were bound to become increasingly bold and simple.

In 1930, when Behrens published a brief review of his work, he omitted all illustrations of the neo-classical buildings of the years before the First World War. Yet it is very likely that Mies was influenced at least as strongly by the revelation of Schinkel's concepts of form as he was by Behrens's excursions into industry. The fundamental principle of classicism – the development of universal solutions, universally applicable to a wide variety of problems – was to interest Mies more and more in years to come.

Behrens's office was an extremely busy place while Mies and Gropius worked there as designers. But if one were to single out two buildings of that period which inspired Mies more than any others, these would have to be the famous Turbine factory for the A.E.G., done in 1909, and the German embassy in St Petersburg, the construction of which was to be supervised by the young Mies. These two buildings showed Behrens at his best and in his two extremes: the first was probably the most important steel-and-glass building prior to Gropius's Fagus factory of 1911; and the second was probably the most accomplished piece of neo-classicism to come out of Behrens's office.

The Turbine factory was a huge hall framed in steel arches spanning some eighty feet and about one hundred feet high at their crowns. These arches were placed about twenty-five feet apart, and the space between, up to the roof-line, was filled with a 'skin' of glass. This great room was planned to be more than 600 feet long, but only a first stage of 400 feet was actually constructed. The corners of the hall were closed off with massive-looking 'piers' of concrete, scored horizontally to contrast with the march of the vertical steel arches along the 400-foot façade. Actually, these concrete corners were quite thin also, and carried no loads. This is a rather significant aspect of the building, for it shows that Behrens – unlike Auguste Perret, for example – was perfectly willing to deviate from structural purism and create an effect by means other than purely functional. Those massive concrete corners of the A.E.G. Turbine factory are a poetic image of strength and power, not a true representation of structural framing. Whether Behrens was justified in using images of this sort in a building whose actual bone structure might have been used to convey the notions of strength and power more convincingly is open to question. Nowadays the sort of imagery practised here by Behrens is often abused by industrial designers to create a suggestion of speed, or power, or uplift, which does not correspond to the reality of structure at all. But these are, of course, decisions dictated largely by taste. In the Behrens building the notion of 'power' was conveyed so convincingly by the great fortress-like concrete corners that no one could possibly have mistaken this structure for anything but what it was. When Mies, many years later, was faced with the problem of how to express a quality of structure despite building-code requirements that forced him to conceal the very structure he was trying to express, he may have thought of Behrens's images of power as a way of conveying the meaning and the content of his buildings.

The German embassy in St Petersburg belonged to the neo-classical category of Behrens's work, and, in retrospect, it does not seem particularly inventive to us today. Its proportions were impressive and noble; its interior finishes were of the finest quality; its sculptural decoration, including an equestrian group over the main-entrance portals, was restrained by comparison with some of the other work of the period. Still, none of this was really very exceptional in a time that saw much more advanced work being done by Wright in America, by the Perrets and Garnier in France, by Gropius and Bruno Taut in Germany.

Yet the St Petersburg embassy contained several spaces of quite extraordinary elegance. If we were able to look at the monumental ground-floor lobby today (unfortunately the building was badly damaged during the Second World War), we would find a space formed almost entirely by regularly spaced columns whose bays were filled with floor-to-ceiling panels of glass. The glass areas (some of them french doors) opened the lobby space out towards a very formal court to the rear of the main building. Elsewhere the columns would become pilasters, holding between them floor-to-ceiling panels of wall area or of doorways – all treated as modular units fitted neatly and tightly between the expressed structural system. Even the grand staircase leading up from the lobby floor was fitted into a column bay and hence treated as an integral part of the structure and the plan of the building. This pattern of verticality imposed upon the building by its expressed column structure was not new to classical architecture; but to Mies it seems to have suggested a way of creating formality and monumentality to which he resorted in several buildings in later years.

When Mies was in Behrens's office he took on several small commissions to carry out on his own. One, a house for Hugo Perls, was in the straight tradition of 'cleaned-up Schinkelism' which Behrens and other German architects of the period employed, generally with good taste, if occasionally with too heavy a hand. The house was two storeys high, quite symmetrical, stuccoed, endowed with a very simple but pronounced cornice line, and a fairly low-pitched tile roof with a low parapet (rather than roof overhangs). Few people passing by the house would give it a second look today; yet anyone willing to take a closer look would find in this house a refinement of proportions, of details, and of simple forms that suggest that its designer was more than a mere follower of Schinkel or of Behrens.

But perhaps the first suggestion of Mies's independent creativeness came in a project done in 1912, a year after the Perls house was completed. For some time Behrens had been working on the design for a truly palatial home to be built for Mme H. E. L. J. Kröller, near

The Hague in Holland. Behrens's design was very Schinkelesque – a two-storey block with a recessed portico topped by a balcony, a pronounced roof cornice suggesting a flat roof, and a partly walled patio to one side. Mme Kröller, the owner of the famous Kröller-Müller collection of modern paintings, went so far as to have Behrens build a full-scale wood-and-canvas model of the house on its intended site. The photographs of this mock-up that still survive show a rather massive and ungainly pile of building blocks, distinguished primarily by the orderliness of its vertical fenestration.

Mies, who had been working on the Kröller job in Behrens's office, went to The Hague in connexion with the construction of the mock-up. For various reasons Mme Kröller decided not to go ahead with the Behrens proposal; instead she asked Mies to stay at The Hague and to design his own version of a house for the same site. Mies stayed at The Hague for a year (he considers time one of the cheapest commodities an architect can spend in the design of a building), and came up with his own version, which was reproduced, full scale in wood and canvas, just as the original Behrens design had been.

The comparison between the two projects is striking. Where Behrens's proposal was a compact, somewhat heavy-looking structure two storeys high throughout, Mies had developed a rather low-slung, extended complex of one-storey wings and colonnades grouped around a central, two-storey-high block facing on to various interior patios [2]. The details were still quite neo-classical, but the massing of the building, with its great, horizontal sweeps of colonnades, was quite

2. *Kröller house project for The Hague, Holland, 1912.* (*Courtesy, Museum of Modern Art*)

different from the tight verticality of a Schinkel building. Unfortunately, this villa never went beyond the mock-up stage either; but its design gave Mies a chance to go beyond Behrens for the first time.

By 1913 Mies returned to Berlin to open his own office. During the eighteen months or so of peace that remained before the outbreak of the First World War, he designed several villas much in the manner of his Perls house three or four years earlier. All were done more or less in the Schinkelesque manner, though the greater use of glass (french doors in particular), the simplification of detail, and the emphasis on fine proportions set his designs apart from similar work done by other architects of those years. Although Mies was still a classicist in terms of form, it was apparent that structure, as an overriding discipline, had begun to interest him more and more. During his year at The Hague he had seen some of the work of H. P. Berlage, the Dutch architect whose unaffected work in brick seemed to Mies to express the material's honest structural possibilities to perfection.

The notion of 'honesty' in structure and structural expression was something that Berlage had acquired from men like Ruskin, who had used the concept initially to attack the pretensions of neo-classicism and eclecticism. Their opposition to those latter evils had, in turn, taken them back to the alleged structural honesty of early medieval architecture. Under the influence of this sort of rationalization Mies became increasingly critical of the surface trappings of Schinkelism. It seemed to him that Behrens and others like him were more interested in form for form's sake, while he was learning, from Berlage, to accept structure as the great, underlying discipline. Some years later Mies put it very clearly when he said: 'We refuse to recognize problems of form, but only problems of building. Form is not the aim of our work, but only the result. Form, by itself, does not exist. Form as an aim is formalism; and that we reject.' Those were brave words – and good words, as far as they went. Just as Behrens had felt the need to cleanse himself of Art Nouveau sentimentality by turning to Schinkel's classicism, so Mies now felt the need to cleanse himself of formalism by finding a moral rationalization of architecture which would, incidentally, determine form, but not be dominated by it. It was a necessary step in Mies's development; and the fact that he was destined one day to swallow some of those words and become one of the first modern architects to return to the creation of eloquent forms does nothing to subtract from the validity of his beliefs in those early days.

THREE

In 1918 Mies returned to Berlin from military service in the German army. He had been an enlisted man in the engineers, building bridges and roads in the Balkans. (Not being a university graduate, he found it impossible to become an officer in the old German army.) Upon his return from the Balkans, Mies found himself in the midst of several revolutions, all taking place simultaneously. First, there was the political revolution – the transfer of power from the Kaiser's defeated empire to the new Weimar Republic. Next, there were political upheavals within republican ranks – all the way from the extreme left, which managed, briefly, to establish Soviet-style dictatorships in several German states, to the near-monarchist right, which was hoping against hope to prepare for the eventual return of the Hohenzollern family to the German throne. But, in the midst of these wild political upheavals, a whole series of upheavals took place in the world of art: there were the German *im*pressionists, holdovers from the prewar years, fighting for a comeback; there were the new *ex*pressionists, very much in vogue though soon to be eclipsed; and there was a sudden influx of ideas from France, Holland, and Russia, all dealing with different aspects of the new Cubist movement. Germany had been completely cut off from these latter developments throughout the war years and, to some extent, even before. Now that the war and the Kaiser were over and done with, now that *any*thing that represented a new point of view could receive a hearing in Germany, the young artists of Mies's generation (he was just over thirty years old) were irresistibly drawn to everything that seemed to represent a new world.

In this exhilarating atmosphere Mies found it possible to make the final, absolute break with the past. He designed one more house in the vaguely classical manner he had developed before 1914; but that house was never built, and it was Mies's last attempt to reconcile neo-classicism with the needs of our time. In the same year in which this last conservative house was designed, Mies produced so radical and

3. Glass office-building project for Berlin, 1919. (Courtesy, Museum of Modern Art)

daring a design for a skyscraper that modern architecture, quite literally, has not been the same since.

The sketches Mies developed in 1919 were for an all-glass tower, twenty storeys in height, with a central core of services from which extended three wings of office spaces, sheathed from street-level to the roof-line with an uninterrupted skin of glass. This sheer cliff of crystal was a staggering piece of imagination and daring in itself [3]; coming from a young man who, only a few months earlier, had been content to design a rather 'safe' and conservative villa in a neo-classical vein, these drawings were almost incomprehensible. For

4. Glass skyscraper project, 1920–1. (Courtesy, Museum of Modern Art)

here, with a single stroke of the pen, as it were, Mies laid the foundation for all the great glass-and-metal skyscrapers we see about us today.

Mies would be the first to admit that this sketch in 1919 was merely the foundation, the beginning, of a vast amount of work on his part and on the part of others. Yet what a beginning, what a step forward! The plan for this building was still oddly fanciful in outline, angular and jagged in shape, rather like an expressionist pattern. The reason for its odd shape, according to Mies, was not any preoccupation with expressionist forms, but, rather, an attempt to study the reflections of light in the many-faceted glass façades of the building. 'I placed the glass walls at slight angles to each other to avoid the monotony of over-large glass surfaces,' Mies wrote. 'I discovered by working with actual glass models that the important thing is the play of reflections and not the effect of light and shadow, as in ordinary buildings.' A year later Mies produced a second set of sketches for another all-glass skyscraper, this one to be thirty storeys high [4 and 5]. It was even more extraordinary than the first one: in plan it consisted of a complex of free forms; each floor was enclosed by a continuous curtain or skin of glass, arranged to follow the compound curves of the outline of the plan. Yet this curved glass skin was made up of dozens of identical flat window units that changed direction on every mullion line, like the sides of a polygon. As a result, the same play of reflections Mies had tried to achieve in the first scheme was carried still farther on the multi-faceted skin of this building. The model of the structure prepared by Mies showed, behind the skin of glass, a stack of reinforced-concrete floor slabs cantilevered out from interior column supports and expressed in a knife-edged metal strip on the glass façade.

Why do these two projects for glass skyscrapers seem so important in retrospect? The answer is in three parts: first, while there had been glassy buildings designed and even constructed before 1919, no proposal had ever been so radically all-glass, so completely uncompromising a statement of what the new technology could produce. Second, the glass skyscrapers were amazingly 'right' for their time – right in terms of their cantilever structure, in terms of their simple, aesthetic expression, in terms of their decisive clarity. And, third, these two projects seem important now because they suddenly pushed Mies into the forefront of the modern movement and assured him a place he has never relinquished since.

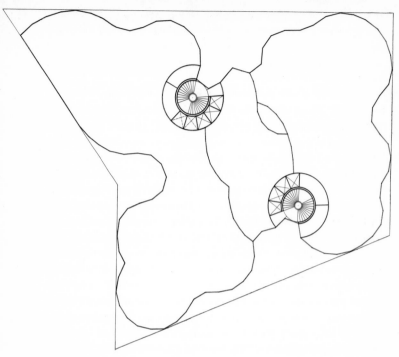

5. Plan of glass skyscraper. (Courtesy, Museum of Modern Art)

For these projects revealed a quality in Mies which has been his most impressive characteristic throughout his career. That quality is the ability to produce architectural statements of such overwhelming precision, simplicity, and single-mindedness that their impact is that of a major revelation. Bold and singlehanded statements have been used for centuries as devices to attract attention to a new dogma or a new personality. But in Mies's case the single-mindedness and precision of his architectural statements has never been meant to attract publicity to his ideas or to himself. (Indeed, Mies is so self-effacing and withdrawn a person that, in the 1940s, his students at the Illinois Institute of Technology once petitioned to have an annual Christmas party at which they might have a chance to meet him!) The startling simplicity of his revelations is, instead, the result of an endless process of purification and crystallization of an idea – until that idea becomes so disarmingly simple, so overwhelmingly 'obvious' that it must, according to Mies's beliefs, represent the ultimate truth. His famous saying – 'less is more' – is not only typical of Mies as a man of few and well-chosen words; it is also descriptive of the method by which he works, a method of distilling ideas to the point of ultimate purity.

As a matter of fact, the logic of Mies's glass towers appears now, in retrospect, almost predictable. Once Mies became disenchanted with formalism and began, through Berlage's work, to think in terms of structural clarity and honesty, it could only be a matter of time for him to investigate the logical consequences of steel, reinforced concrete, and glass, and to arrive at a statement of 'honesty' as he saw it when applied to those new materials. To him the answer was perfectly clear; steel and concrete represented strength; these would be the 'bones' of his buildings. Glass was a shimmering veil that could be draped over the skeleton to form the 'skin'. Gropius and Behrens had, of course, done steel-and-glass buildings; but their structures showed the 'bones' clearly on the exterior, with glass used as a fill-in panel set into the spaces between the structural skeleton. In Mies's skyscraper projects the bones and skin became completely separated – the skeleton inside, the skin of glass outside – so that there was no possible visual confusion between what supported the floor and roof loads and what kept out the weather. 'Skin and bone construction' is what Mies called it, and the description has stuck.

Despite his relative isolation, Mies was undoubtedly influenced by certain movements in painting and sculpture which swept across Europe in the years immediately after the First World War; and the qualities found in his glass-tower projects were present in some of these movements as well. For example, the Russian Suprematist painter, Kasimir Malevich, in his famous *White on White* (now in the permanent collection of the Museum of Modern Art) had made the same sort of uncompromising statement about painting which Mies was to make about architecture with his glass towers a couple of years later. For just as Malevich's painting was, in effect, a clean slate offered to the world, to receive an entirely new set of images, so Mies's glassy façades were giant mirrors held up to the world to reflect an entirely new set of forms. And Mies had seen, too, how the Russian Constructivists like Lissitzky and Tatlin, in their mechanistic sculpture of the same period, always articulated different parts of a structure, both by separating the parts and by making them of different materials. Mies, like everyone else of his generation, was conscious of these movements abroad: exhibitions were held in Berlin of Suprematist and Constructivist painting and sculpture, and Mies became a member of the Novembergruppe – an organization of artists in many fields interested in finding a channel through which to bring their work to the attention of the public. (The November-gruppe was generally left-wing in its politics, having been named after the month in 1918 which saw the revolution that created the Weimar Republic.) Mies, as head of the architectural section of the November-gruppe, helped arrange several exhibitions of advanced architectural projects, and his own two skyscraper proposals were first shown within that context.

In a sense, the idea that Mies should associate himself with a movement motivated – in part, at least – by political objectives seems odd. His own political inclinations are practically non-existent; on at least one occasion, during the years after the Second World War, when told by a friend that another German architect of some promin-ence – who, unlike Mies, had remained in Germany during the Hitler period – had received an important post despite his past Nazi con-nexions, Mies flared up angrily, saying, in effect, that he didn't give a damn about the man's politics, but *was* concerned with the fact that the man was a rotten architect! Mies's own personal tastes – his preferences for quiet, expensive clothes, for restrained but near-precious building materials – seem to have led him in later years into associations with wealthy conservatives rather than Bohemian radicals. Still, in the years following the end of the Kaiser's Reich it was simply not possible to be an avant-garde artist without becoming associated with left-wing republicans. Mies, of course, didn't care, just so long as his fellow artists were good – as artists . . .

Mies's next project – an office building of reinforced concrete and glass [6] – was also exhibited by the Novembergruppe. It was a design startlingly different from the rather exuberant free forms of the two glass towers; for here Mies took the most rational plan form, the pure rectangle, and framed it with a regularly spaced grid of reinforced-concrete columns. These, in turn, carried concrete floor-slabs that were cantilevered out beyond the face of the outside columns and turned up to form continuous, concrete parapets at each floor-level. Above each parapet and reaching up to the floor-slab above, Mies placed ribbon windows that ran, uninterrupted, around the perimeter of the building.

Today this starkly horizontal structure seems very familiar; in

6. *Concrete office-building project, 1922. The entrance portico is seen at left.*
(*Courtesy, Museum of Modern Art*)

debased form it has been built in most large American cities. But, in the
year 1922, when Mies designed this austere and uncompromising
structure, its form was anything but familiar. Eric Mendelsohn, who
was perhaps more directly influenced by this project than any other
architect of the period, did not build his famous ribbon-window
department store for Schocken, in Chemnitz, until six years later;
and Peter Behrens did not take up the theme until 1935, in his tobacco
factory at Linz, Austria. Since then, of course, the ribbon-window
building with cantilevered floor slabs around the periphery has
become the single most commonly used office structure in the world.

Unfortunately, most of Mies's imitators never really investigated
his 1922 project as closely as they might have done. For Mies
incorporated in it several ideas that are worth exploring further. For
example, there was more than one good reason for making this
building a strong horizontal structure: first, of course, there was
Mies's feeling that reinforced concrete lent itself uncommonly well to
this sort of cantilevered structure, and that cantilevers, being the
projection of horizontal elements beyond the vertical column frame,

tended to create horizontal rather than vertical patterns. Still, in his two glass towers Mies had used cantilevered floor-slabs also; yet the exterior expression of the glass skin had been a series of closely spaced, vertical mullions dividing the glass and running the full height of the building, from sidewalk to roof-line. Theoretically, Mies might have done the same thing in his 1922 project; yet he chose, instead, to make this building an uncompromisingly horizontal composition.

The reason is really quite simple: while the glass towers were to be twenty and thirty storeys in height, respectively, the 1922 building was going to be only eight storeys high. Its proportions were going to be largely horizontal in any event; therefore Mies felt that it was necessary to underline the horizontal nature of the building rather than fight it with a vertically patterned skin of glass. Many of the ribbon-window buildings we see nowadays in New York or Chicago are twenty or thirty storeys high, with the result that the horizontal emphasis of the ribbon pattern is at disturbing odds with the vertical 'soar' of the building mass. It was perfectly obvious to Mies that no building could be a clear statement unless its proportions and detail were related, from the smallest unit to the over-all form.

Out of his decision to make this a horizontal building, Mies developed a second set of details which have been largely ignored by his imitators. In a vertical building, Mies felt, it was possible to let the verticals rise straight up into the sky, without cutting them off in any formal fashion. (Louis Sullivan's 'cap', terminating the vertical ascent of his expressed columns, always seemed a little incongruous, especially as Sullivan knew that the only way to stop his soaring verticals was to make the cap a heavy 'lid' to hold down the building . . .) But a horizontal building, Mies saw, needed a definite horizontal line to terminate the sweep of ribbons, and it had to be decidedly different from the ribbons below it. Mies's slim-edged roof-slab on top of the 1922 building was a simple and convincing answer.

Finally, there was the problem of how to get into a horizontal building. (It is a matter of constant bafflement to the average layman that architects find it so hard to design entrances; yet this is just about the most difficult aesthetic problem in the development of any building.) In Mies's horizontal structure, there was no way of inserting a meaningful entrance without interrupting the pattern of the horizontal ribbons in some manner. Most architects would have cut into the horizontal pattern with a heavily framed entrance rectangle, hoping that no one would pay too much attention to the violation of formal

31

and structural principle involved. Mies, as usual, cut the Gordian knot by simply interrupting his first-floor ribbon for the width of the entrance lobby. The width of the entrance was not framed in any way; instead, the gap between the horizontal ribbons was filled with a rather monumental (and classical) flight of steps revealing for the first time the great concrete columns recessed behind the façade of the building. No better and more direct way of entering a horizontal ribbon building has been discovered since.

Here, as in the glass towers, there emerges something of Mies which has set him apart from most of his contemporaries. The fundamental concept of the building is, as usual, astonishing in its simplicity. Yet, beyond the seemingly 'obvious' simplicity of the concept, there appear a host of carefully developed details as unobtrusive as the fine stitching on a well-tailored suit, but just as important. 'God,' Mies likes to say, 'is in the details.' He says it only half-jokingly.

Shortly after Mies completed his design for the ribbon-window building, he produced two other projects of far-reaching importance. Like the glass towers and the office building, these two projects – a brick villa and a concrete villa – were never built. They, too, were first exhibited by the Novembergruppe, and, like the earlier projects, can be traced in part to outside influences in the related arts.

As a matter of fact, Mies has always denied that he was influenced directly by painting or sculpture. 'One day, when Henry-Russell Hitchcock [the well-known critic and historian] came to see me,' Mies once said, 'he was surprised to see my collection of Klee paintings. He was sure that I would have some Mondrians on my walls!' However that may be, the painters, sculptors, and architects of Mondrian's persuasion – all members of the Dutch De Stijl group – *did* exhibit in Berlin in the early 1920s, and the leader of the De Stijl movement, Theo van Doesburg, had visited Berlin regularly from 1922 on. So it is at least possible that Mies's extraordinarily linear and asymmetrically composed plans for the two villas were influenced by the interlocking lines, squares, and rectangles of De Stijl painting. Indeed, the brick villa, with its interlocking rectangular glass and brick volumes, looks very much like a De Stijl sculpture by Vantongerloo; and the plan is clearly reminiscent of Mondrian's early paintings. All of this work was well known to Mies. In 1923 he and the De Stijl abstractionist, Hans Richter (who worked primarily with films), had begun to produce the magazine *G* – a publication devoted to all the arts. (*G* stood for the German word *Gestaltung*, creative action.) And Mies, being primarily involved in exhibition design, saw all the exhibitions of De Stijl and Russian Constructivism that reached Germany.

Yet Mies was also bitterly opposed to formalism.

We reject all aesthetic speculation, all doctrine, all formalism [he wrote in the first issue of *G*]. Architecture is the will of an epoch translated into space; living, changing, new . . . To create form out of the nature of our tasks with the methods of our time – *this is our task*.

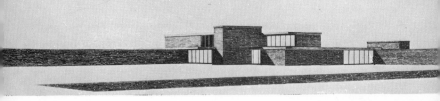

7. Brick villa project, 1923. The centre is a cluster of brick and glass. From this centre extend long walls of brick that reach out towards the landscape. (Courtesy, Museum of Modern Art)

In other words, he not only rejected the De Stijl formalism as an influence (just as he rejected the then rampant expressionism as an influence), he actively opposed both; and his published writings of the period prove that this is no wishful afterthought on Mies's part today. Still, the graphic means employed by Mies to present his projects, especially in the plan drawings, are strongly reminiscent of the graphic means developed by De Stijl artists.

Much more fundamental was the influence of architects like Berlage and Frank Lloyd Wright. Mies had seen the great Wright exhibition that came to Berlin in 1910. 'The dynamic impulse emanating from Wright's work invigorated a whole generation,' he wrote later. The brick villa, especially, shows how strongly Mies felt that 'dynamic impulse'. The building is planned exactly like a typical Wrightian country house [7]: a core of rooms, screened from one another, but also partly open to one another to permit the easy flow of space between them; and an extension of this core of rooms far out into the landscape by means of long walls that reach out from the interior all the way into the surrounding gardens. This general principle had been followed by Wright in many of his early houses during the first decade of the century. Although the principle was sometimes obscured – because Wright tended to be fussy and ornate in his details – it was none the less visible to a trained eye. What Mies did with this principle is almost as astonishing as what he had done with Behrens's neo-classicism a few years earlier: with a single stroke of the pen he brought Wright up to date and made him modern! The plan of the brick villa, done in 1923, is in fact a preview of the sort of simple and strong statement which Wright himself was to make with his Usonian houses of the 1930s.

In its plastic composition, however, the brick villa owed very little to Wright. Its brick nature seemed to suggest to Mies the sort of blocky, squared-off composition which Berlage had handled to perfection. In a way the villa is an extension of brick-building – masses and volumes formed by bricks and interlocking much in the way in which bricks interlock. Although the brick villa was a radical statement for its time (especially as no avant-gardist worth his salt would have seriously thought of building with as old-fashioned a material as brick!), it now seems somewhat dated in everything but its dynamic, entirely modern plan.

The concrete villa [8] Mies designed in the following year has none of this dated look. In plan composition it owes something to Wright, although the courts and formal pedestals (with formal flights of steps) show that Mies never forgot the valuable lessons he learned from Schinkel. But, in structure and form, this villa is a typically Miesian statement, clear and precise, and unmistakably of reinforced concrete. There are great, sweeping cantilevers, long ribbons of glass, corner windows, and deep roof overhangs. There is a dynamic quality in this building which not only spells 'reinforced concrete' to perfection, but also seems to suggest some sort of 'American' style. Where the brick villa, despite its expanding, pinwheel-shaped plan, seemed rather tight and confined in its volumes, the concrete villa is an expanding organism that somehow suggests a spacious continent. Its wings, arranged in a modified S-shaped pattern, separate areas of different

8. *Concrete villa project, 1924. Different elements of the plan are clearly articulated. (Courtesy, Museum of Modern Art)*

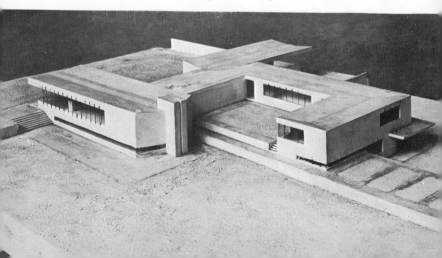

function much as the 'articulated' house plans of today try to do. Although it was never built, the concrete villa had an influence upon some of Mies's contemporaries comparable to the inflence of his ribbon-window building. It looks so familiar and modern to us today because it is so similar to the kind of house made popular in California by men like Richard Neutra.

By the end of 1924 Mies had not built a single important modern building. The very precarious economic and political situation in Germany, with its wild inflationary cycles and its severe unemployment, had greatly curtailed building activities throughout the country. Mies and others of his generation built very little during those early years after the First World War; indeed, most of their work consisted of projects that were published, exhibited, widely discussed, and discarded. To 'practical men', Mies's projects seemed of questionable value; but, among avant-gardists, Mies's concepts, with their enormous precision and clarity of statement, were greatly admired. Still, the acid test was yet to come: would Mies be able to build what he preached? A contemporary writer on architecture spoke condescendingly of Mies as having made some 'valuable suggestions', and hoped that his 'beautiful, idealistic projects' would withstand the 'fire of practicality'. He need not have worried; the only obstacle Mies has ever had to face is the obstacle of an outdated, outdistanced technology.

By 1925 Mies's astonishing and well-publicized projects made him sufficiently known so that private and public clients began to come to him more and more often. He built several brick-and-glass villas for wealthy businessmen in the fashionable suburbs of Berlin and in the Rhineland, while at the same time constructing a monument to the German Communist leaders, Karl Liebknecht and Rosa Luxemburg, and designing a low-cost housing project for the City of Berlin. Although none of these structures had the daring of his glass towers, they all revealed Mies to be, in all likelihood, the best *builder* among the modernists of his generation. The brickwork used in his elegant villas can be compared only to some sort of inlaid mosaic of precious stones. (Mies often went down to the kilns to make a painstaking selection of the bricks he wanted before they were shipped to any of his jobs.) Indeed, the villas were designed with infinite care so that all the dimensions would be multiples of the standard brick dimension, with the result that no 'fudging' of edges or openings occurred anywhere.

Although some modernists in Europe had begun to use brick by 1925, most of Mies's contemporaries insisted upon using smooth surfaces of stucco in the hopes of achieving the sort of 'Machine Art' effects that were so popular with Le Corbusier and Gropius. Actually, these surfaces were little more than a pretence, for behind the skin of stucco most architects concealed a traditional wall of concrete block. Still, everyone was hoping to see the great day when industry would produce large, smoothly finished sheets of building materials in modular dimensions, so that architects could assemble their structures using big building components rather than the small-scale stones and bricks of the past. The hope became father to the completed building, and the typically modern house or store of 1925 was a smoothly surfaced affair that looked as if it had rolled off the assembly line – although, in reality, it had been put together by the same old-fashioned building methods used by every architect for a hundred years and more. The only difference was that, as the surfaces were smooth rather than patterned, every streak and other blemish began to show almost immediately!

In his purist attitude towards structure, Mies rebelled against this sort of sham. He was convinced that only an architecture honestly arrived at by the explicit use of available building materials could be justified in moral terms. Because brick and brick masons were available, he built brick houses. But, because he, better than most of those who paid lip-service to industrialized building, knew what this could mean to architecture, he insisted in his brick-bonding upon a degree of precision that tended to impose even upon the *craft* of brick-building all the discipline of industrialized construction. For Mies saw it very clearly indeed.

I consider the industrialization of building methods the key problem of the day [Mies said in 1924]. Once we succeed in this, our social, economic, technical and even artistic problems will be easy to solve. How can industrialization be carried out? ... The problem before us is [to effect] a revolution in the whole nature of the building industry. The nature of the building process will not change as long as we employ essentially the same [traditional] building materials, for they require manual labour ... Our first consideration, therefore, must be to find a new building material ... It must be a light material which not only permits but requires industrial production. All the [building] parts will be made in a factory and the work at the site will consist only of assemblage, requiring extremely few man-hours ... I am convinced that traditional methods of construction will disappear. In case anyone regrets that the house of the future can no longer be made by hand workers, he should remember that the automobile is no longer manufactured by carriage-makers.

All very familiar to us today, some thirty-five years later. But in 1924 Mies's clear perception of the central practical issues facing the building industry – and architecture – was remarkable, to say the least. For Mies was really drawing up, in those few words, a precise prescription for exactly the sort of building panel that modern industry is now, at long last, beginning to mass-produce: a plastic or light-weight metal panel designed to be bolted together on the job so rapidly that in 1955 a twenty-five-storey office building in Manhattan could be completely enclosed with such panels in a matter of twelve hours – or, to use Mies's prescription of 1924 again: 'the work at the site will consist only of assemblage, requiring extremely few man-hours'.

Meanwhile, until such building materials were available, Mies felt that the traditional ones would have to do the job. 'The old brick masonry has many advantages,' he said. And indeed it has; one of the most important is that it weathers well if handled properly. Few avant-garde houses built in Europe in the early 1920s have stood the test of time as well as those built by Mies. His traditional training, his experience both in his father's shop and on building sites in the Rhineland, had served him extremely well; for he was one of the few modernists who was not a *theoretical* architect, but a master builder with experience firmly rooted in the past.

It is not his traditional building experience alone that has served Mies well throughout his career. It is also his early training, in Behrens's office and before, in the classical tradition. It was fashionable in the 1920s (as it is today) to scoff at the academies and to deny the validity of their teaching. Yet the traditionalists knew (and the few surviving ones still know) a good deal about architecture which the modernists could study with considerable profit. They knew not only how to get their buildings to weather well, to stand the test of time; they also knew how to relate their buildings to one another and to the landscape around them. Many Americans, having heard Louis Sullivan's and Frank Lloyd Wright's laments about the 1893 Chicago exhibition, in which the disciples of the Paris Beaux Arts Academy stifled the exuberant sprouts of a new and originally American architecture, now equate the Beaux Arts with the devil. Yet the Chicago exhibition, for all its fakery, had unity; all its component buildings related to one another; their cornices all lined up; the progression from space to space, from level to level, indoors and, just as importantly, outdoors, was carefully studied. Compared to the hideous shambles of the Brussels World's Fair of 1958, Chicago was a dream of planning and of unity.

The most impressive quality possessed by Mies's early modern villas – apart from their precision of detail, their large and simple areas of glass, their daring concrete roof cantilevers, and their openness in interior planning – is their classical serenity of setting. The first radical houses built by Le Corbusier, Gropius, Breuer, and others often seemed to be almost dropped out of the sky to settle where they might in the landscape. Mies's houses, on the other hand, are always sited on terraces, surrounded by retaining walls, reached by means of short, easy, almost monumental flights of steps. They look as though they belonged in their setting from the day they were completed. Wright, who was the past master of siting a building in the country, used other than classical means to achieve that same sense of belonging. Mies, a classicist in spirit though not in practice, adapted the devices of Schinkel and of those who inspired Schinkel to achieve a similar effect.

Knowledge of how to build and of how to place the building, and a calm, self-assured, instinctive knowledge of what was truly 'modern' and what was a passing fad – these qualities have made Mies's houses of the 1920s almost timeless. Where much of Corbu's work of the same years has the charm, in retrospect, of a brilliant period piece, Mies's houses of those days might well be built in the 1950s by anyone sufficiently well-to-do to afford such perfect workmanship.

The monument [9] to the martyred German Communist leaders, Karl Liebknecht and Rosa Luxemburg, was built of brick also. It was a composition of superimposed and cantilevered masses of masonry, somewhat like Vantongerloo's De Stijl sculpture, but, unlike it, very structural in feeling. (In Vantongerloo's compositions the rectangular masses always interlocked to create a play of forms almost equally valid regardless of which side was 'up'; whereas Mies's monument was an assembly of massive, rectangular 'slabs', one always resting upon the one below, each cantilevered out from a clearly defined base, or recessed above a similarly defined projecting plane.)

In some respects Mies's monument is much closer to Wright's Larkin building in Buffalo, done in 1904, or to certain details in Wright's Robie house in Chicago, built in 1908, though here again, as in his brick-villa project, Mies seemed to 'modernize' Wright by stripping the latter's dynamic forms of all superfluous, Art Nouveau trimmings. Indeed, there almost seems to have been an unconscious give-and-take between Wright and Mies during the 1920s and 1930s: for the Liebknecht–Luxemburg monument of 1926, while based in part upon Wright's earliest work, also appears like a preview of Wright's most famous house, 'Falling Water', at Bear Run, Pennsylvania, the stunning composition of planes and cantilevers jutting out over a waterfall.

As recently as 1957 the U.S. State Department was deeply disturbed that Mies's 'dossier' contained evidence of his having built a monument to two German Communists. Mies, with characteristic honesty, never tried to explain away this excursion into political architecture. To him, people are admirable when they hold deep convictions and act according to them. Needless to say, Mies has never tried to ignore the quality of such convictions: his dealings with the Nazi charlatans are clear evidence of his deep-seated moral sense. But, what was the quality of Liebknecht's and Luxemburg's convictions when judged,

9. Monument to Karl Liebknecht and Rosa Luxemburg, Berlin, 1926. The massing of horizontal forms foreshadows some of Wright's later houses. The monument is a thick wall treated as a massive relief. (Courtesy, Museum of Modern Art)

not in retrospect or in the light of today's experience with Soviet imperialism, but in the light of the German revolution against the Kaiser and against the Kaiser's war? To Mies, and to many of his contemporaries, Karl Liebknecht and Rosa Luxemburg stood for social justice, for economic as well as political democracy, for planning, for peace – in short, for all the things the Kaiser's Germany had more or less denied its citizens. Mies felt then (and feels today) that these two Communist leaders held honest convictions and lived according to them. He was not particularly interested in their party allegiances; he was interested only in their moral calibre. When they were assassinated by extremists of the Right, Mies felt honoured to be chosen to build their monument. No one can tell where Liebknecht and Luxemburg would have stood after the great Soviet purges of the 1930s, after the Hitler–Stalin pact, after the rape of Hungary. To judge Mies or anyone else by political criteria established in retrospect is obviously preposterous, and it is to the credit of the State Department that it has apparently reversed itself and awarded Mies the commission of building the new U.S. Consulate at São Paulo, Brazil, thus certifying him as politically pure.

Although Mies was to return to brick masonry frequently in later years, the completion of the brick villas and the brick monument were a distinct milestone in his career. He was now sufficiently well known to be appointed, in 1926, first Vice-President of the Deutsche Werkbund – the organization that, in 1914, had given Gropius his chance to build the glass-and-steel exhibition structure in Cologne. The Werkbund had been founded by a group of architects, artists, and industrialists to attempt to achieve an integration of art and industry in order to raise the level of German product design. Mies's elevation to the effective leadership of the Werkbund at that time was to prove of tremendous importance to the future of modern architecture; for the organization was about to hold its second major exhibition at Stuttgart, and Mies was appointed Director of that effort. What he did with the Stuttgart exhibition advanced the popular cause of architecture more decisively than any other single event of the 1920s.

SIX

The significance of the Werkbund exhibition in Stuttgart was twofold: first, it represented a kind of summary of the total achievement of modern European architecture and furniture design up to that moment, and suggested some of the future potentialities of the movement. And, second, it told something about the qualities of its Director – Ludwig Mies van der Rohe – who, as first Vice-President of the Werkbund, had been put in charge of this extraordinary undertaking.

If Le Corbusier or Frank Lloyd Wright had been placed in a similar position, the chances are that the Weissenhof development would have been a one-man exhibition – admittedly exciting, but, still, a vehicle for the propagation of a single point of view. Mies, self-effacing as he is, did the almost inconceivable: he laid down the general ground-rules for the exhibition, and then threw the whole exhibition open to every modern European architect of any note! And even the ground-rules laid down by Mies were liberal in the extreme. 'I have refrained from laying down a rigid programme,' he explained, 'in order to leave each individual as free as possible to carry out his ideas. In drawing up the general plan I felt it important to avoid regulations that might interfere with free expression.' Mies's first 'general plan' was quite prophetic of today's most advanced city-planning concepts: he proposed to have all circulation *within* the Weissenhof limited to pedestrians, and to provide parking facilities for motor-cars along the perimeter of the development. This, however, implied some sort of central ownership and control of the whole area, and the City of Stuttgart found it necessary to have the Weissenhof exhibition designed in such a way that each building could, eventually, be sold to an individual owner. To facilitate this, Mies adjusted his site plan to provide through-streets and individual parking areas for each residential unit

There were thirty-three of these residential units in all, some of them were single-family houses, others were apartment blocks containing as many as twenty-four flats. In drawing up the list of participants, Mies showed a high degree of discrimination: almost every modern European architect of importance was included, although several of them had not achieved their present recognition when Mies made his choice. In addition to Le Corbusier and his cousin, Pierre Jeanneret, Mies invited Gropius; J. J. P. Oud, the leading Dutch architect of the De Stijl group; Victor Bourgeois, the Belgian modernist who had produced some rather fantastic city-planning projects during the first decades of the century; Bruno Taut, Hans Poelzig, and Peter Behrens – all of them German pioneer architects whose work is still in high regard today; Hans Scharoun, whose strikingly individualistic style has dominated German architecture throughout the years since the end of the Second World War; and several others. Eric Mendelsohn was invited, but was unable to participate. Mies himself designed a long apartment block.

The scope of the Weissenhof development was remarkable. Here was a full-scale exhibition concerned with the most advanced theories of construction and design, and financed by a relatively small provincial city and an association of artists and industrialists – all operating in a defeated and impoverished nation! Nothing comparable has been done since in any other country; several attempts to duplicate the Weissenhof experiment in the U.S. failed because no one in the U.S. building industry has had sufficient vision or guts to put up the required funds – even temporarily! More than thirty years after it was built, the Weissenhof exhibition is still unique – a remarkable testimony to the vision and courage of a nation and its industry.

Mies had a very clear idea of what the Weissenhof experiment ought to achieve.

In spite of its technical and economic aspects, the problem of the modern dwelling is primarily one of building-art [he said]. It is a complex problem of planning and can therefore be solved only by creative minds, not by calculation or organization. Therefore, I feel it imperative, in spite of current talk about 'rationalization' and 'standardization', to keep the project from being one-sided or doctrinaire. I have therefore invited leading representatives of the modern movement to make their contribution . . .

The different contributions varied both in quality and in emphasis: Corbu's two buildings have been described in a previous volume; they were perhaps the most imaginative structures at the Weissenhof. Gropius built two houses made entirely of prefabricated wall and roof panels, equipped with prefabricated storage walls and furnished with Marcel Breuer's airy tubular-steel chairs. These two houses remain the

10. *Street side of Weissenhof apartments. The ribbon windows do not conceal the column structure.* (*Courtesy, Museum of Modern Art*)

most rational statement of prefabrication to have been achieved to date, and no prefabricated house built since the Weissenhof opened in 1927 has gone very far beyond Gropius's remarkable demonstration. When Gropius turned seventy, in 1953, a party was given for him in Chicago at which Mies, who is usually the most taciturn guest at any such occasion, rose to make what must have been the longest speech of his career. 'I am glad I had once the possibility in Stuttgart to give Gropius a hand so that he could demonstrate his ideas on industrialization and prefabrication,' Mies said, among other things. 'He built two houses there which were the most interesting ones in the exhibition.' As usual, Mies was being excessively modest, for his own block of apartments was a beautiful and clear-cut achievement as well [10 and 11]: steel-framed, finished in stucco, topped with sheltered roof gardens, and endowed with long bands of glass and prefabricated partitions and storage walls, this block would be remarkable in any development of garden apartments put up in the 1950s. By no means other than perfectionist detail and perfect proportion, Mies succeeded

11. Apartment house at the Weissenhof exhibition, 1927. Garden side of block, showing sheltered roof terraces. (Courtesy, Museum of Modern Art)

in creating one of the best housing units put up in Europe in the 1920s. Indeed, the only comparable structure of its type at the Weissenhof was the strip of five terrace houses by Oud – a demonstration of small-scale housing which continues to influence planners to this day.

The Weissenhof exhibition was an important event in the history of modern furniture design as well. Probably the most famous and most widely used chair designed since the First World War is the so-called tubular-steel 'cantilever chair' – a chair whose profile is, roughly, S-shaped, and whose frame consists of a continuous steel tube. It is today a familiar staple in every restaurant from Bangkok to New York.

The history of this particular chair is full of twists and turns, and full of bitter conflicts – all of which, somehow, culminated at the Weissenhof exhibition. The first man to use tubular steel for the frames of chairs and tables was the young Hungarian-born architect Marcel Breuer, who had been put in charge of the furniture workshop at Gropius's famous design school – the Bauhaus – in 1924 when he was only twenty-two years old. Sometime in 1925 Breuer, who used to ride around on a bicycle in those days, realized that the tubing that formed the handlebars of his bicycle could be bent into more complex shapes to form the supports for pieces of furniture. He approached the manufacturers of this sort of tubing to obtain their assistance in the development of a few experimental chairs. Like many practical men faced with a new idea, the manufacturers thought the designer was mad, but finally consented; and Breuer began to produce a whole series of chairs and tables of elegantly curved steel tubing, with seats and backs formed of stretched canvas or caning, and table tops formed of polished plywood slabs screwed to the tubular frame.

The best and simplest of Breuer's tubular-steel inventions was undoubtedly a little stool whose continuous frame, in profile, looked like an upside-down letter U, and whose top was either of stretched canvas or of wood – depending upon whether the piece was to be used for sitting on, or as an occasional table. This stool was mass-produced for the new Bauhaus buildings designed and built by Gropius in Dessau in 1926. When these buildings were nearing completion, the Dutch architect, Mart Stam (who was also to be represented at the Weissenhof in 1927), came to visit the Bauhaus, and Breuer showed him around. When they came to the U-shaped stools, Breuer picked up one of them, set it down on its side, so that it seemed to 'kneel' on one side of the U, and said: 'That's going to be my next chair!' Mart Stam, who was doing some tubular-steel furniture of his own at the time, may or may not have remembered the incident. In any event, shortly after Stam returned to Rotterdam from Dessau, he produced an S-shaped cantilever chair remarkably similar to the 'kneeling' version of Breuer's U-shaped stool. It was a rather crude affair, consisting of straight lengths of plumber's pipe with elbow connexions at all corners, rather than continuous tubing. To the 'kneeling' U shape was added an extra length of pipe to form the back.

While all this was going on, Mies had been working quietly and independently on a cantilever chair of his own [12 and 13] – a similarly curved frame based on much the same principle both Breuer and Stam seemed to be exploring. However, Mies's chair was the first of the three to be completed, and a patent was issued to Mies which assured him of royalties on the basic design for years to come. As a matter of fact, it is highly unlikely that Mies had been influenced by Breuer's chairs and tables, except in so far as Breuer had been the first to use chromium-plated tubular steel for furniture. Mies's chairs

12. Original 'cantilever chair', designed in 1926. (Courtesy, Museum of Modern Art)

were quite different in profile from the almost angular S-shapes arrived at by Stam and Breuer; *his* had the slow, graceful curve of a Brancusi sculpture and the ample width of Mies himself. Moreover, unlike the Stam and Breuer models, Mies's chairs, though exceedingly beautiful, had a disconcerting tendency to tip forward and propel the sitter across the room as he or she tried to get out of the chair. A later adjustment helped to fix that.

At the Weissenhof, Stam exhibited his own rather clumsy S-chairs; Mies exhibited his very suave and elegant S-chairs; and Breuer (who furnished Gropius's houses) could only show some of his many early, revolutionary tubular-steel chairs and tables, but not his own version of the S-chair, which, in fact, was not to appear on the market until the following year. It was a tragic thing for Breuer, who had done all the pioneering in this field: not only was his best design to be developed

13. Another version of the cantilever chair, this time constructed of flat, chromium-plated bars of steel, 1930. (Courtesy, Museum of Modern Art)

by others first, but – to make matters even worse – *his* version of the S-chair turned out to be the one that is still mass-produced the world over, and at no profit to himself. Only Mies ever obtained a mechanical patent on the basic idea of a cantilever chair, and Mies's S-chairs, because of their fairly high cost and somewhat impractical (though beautiful) performance, were never really mass-produced at all!

Despite this little storm in a teacup, the Weissenhof development in the hills above Stuttgart was a huge success. A handsome book on the development was published by the Werkbund, and each architect explained his contribution in detail. Mies, the man of few words, had built the largest structure in the exhibition and, characteristically, contributed the briefest statement in the book – twelve lines of tight-lipped prose, entitled 'About My Block', as opposed to some 200 lines of descriptive matter by Gropius explaining his small, prefabricated units. Each word in Mies's statement reads as if it had been put down under extreme duress, and the whole statement could hardly have been drier or more reserved. His contention that 'less is more' has always provided Mies with a perfect excuse for cutting short his own public statements.

Perhaps the finest compliment paid to the Weissenhof was unconsciously contributed by the Nazis, who singled out the development as a prime example of Kulturbolschewismus and Degenerate Architecture. One of the first 'cultural' acts performed by the Nazis after they came to power in 1933 was to print photo-montage picture postcards of the Weissenhof showing its streets populated by Arabs and their camels. The montage and its caption – 'Arab Village, Stuttgart' – was meant to convey the depths of depravity to which the Weimar Republic's architects had descended. Next, the guardians of German culture put pitched roofs on top of the flat-roofed Weissenhof structures, thus infusing them with a shot of Blood and Soil. Still, the development was almost recognizable until Allied air-raids did serious damage to some of the structures (and especially the glass walls) during the Second World War. After that, the window openings were bricked or boarded up, or narrowed down in size to preserve precious heat during the winter. By 1945 the Weissenhof was but a hollow and deformed shell of its former self. In the late 1950s, however, efforts were under way to restore the Werkbund's spectacular achievement to its former glory. The Bonn Republic's first President, Theodor Heuss, had once headed the Werkbund and now saw to it that the Werkbund's finest achievement was salvaged for posterity.

SEVEN

The success of the Weissenhof exhibition gave Mies considerable standing among modern architects in Germany, so that when the time came for the German government to select an architect to design its Pavilion for the 1929 International exhibition in Barcelona, Mies was chosen to do the job.

The first thing that needs to be said about the Barcelona Pavilion is that it is considered by many – to this day – the most beautiful modern building to have been constructed anywhere [14–18]. This is so for several reasons: first, Mies decided that the German exhibit was going to be the Pavilion itself, not something displayed inside it. (After all, who could remember what had been exhibited inside Paxton's Crystal Palace, or inside Sullivan's Transportation building at the Chicago Fair in 1893?) As a result, there were practically no functional

14. Main approach to Barcelona Pavilion. Walls at right are of green Tinian marble. (Courtesy, Mies van der Rohe)

requirements worth mentioning, so that the Pavilion could, in fact, be a pure exercise in spatial composition. Second, there was the fact that money seems to have been no object: somehow, Mies was able to specify Roman travertine, Tinian marble, grey transparent glass, onyx, chromium-plated steel columns – in short, the most precious materials available to any architect. And, finally, there was Mies's phenomenal display of genius. No doubt the Barcelona Pavilion showed the usual 'influences' – some stronger than others. But it showed, above all, the hand of an artist of such elegance and perfection that no modern building put up since – except, perhaps, one or two of Mies's later works – has been able to escape invidious comparisons with the detailing of this lovely structure!

Here, at last, was the fulfilment of the promise of Mies's glass-tower projects. Here was the tangible evidence of the genius that had lain dormant during the years of the well-proportioned, well-built (but rather dry) brick villas and stucco apartments. Here, at last, was the emergence of a master equal in every way to Wright and to Le Corbusier – a master with so sure a hand that no one would ever again be able to question his prowess.

The Barcelona Pavilion was a small, one-storey jewel of a building placed upon a wide pedestal of travertine, part of which held a pool lined in black glass. The building itself consisted of a sweeping, horizontal roof-plane supported on eight chromium-plated steel columns, cross-shaped in section (rather than H-shaped like most standard steel columns). Below this roof, there was a rectangular composition of glass and marble walls that formed a series of beautiful spaces, all

15. Plan of Barcelona Pavilion, 1929. Shaded areas are pools lined with black glass. (Courtesy, Mies van der Rohe)

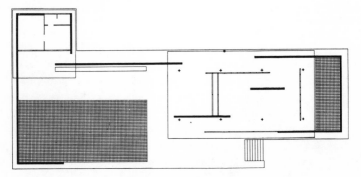

16. Pool and principal exhibition area of Barcelona Pavilion. (Courtesy, Museum of Modern Art)

open to one another and open to various outdoor areas beyond the glass. The only objects shown inside these spaces were several elegant chairs and tables especially designed by Mies. The glass walls were divided by slim, vertical bars of chromium-plated steel; some of the glass was a transparent grey (a shade in increasing use in American buildings since 1945 to reduce sky glare); other walls were of etched glass, two sheets back to back, with light sources between the glass sheets to make the wall a brilliantly luminous panel.

In their asymmetrical, rectilinear composition, the walls of the Barcelona Pavilion looked in plan very much like a De Stijl painting. In the third dimension, the building had some of the sweep of Wright's Robie house. And the pedestal seemed reminiscent of Schinkel's neo-classicism. Yet, even if these influences were present (and they probably were), Mies improved upon each of them: Van Doesburg never painted as beautiful a composition as the Barcelona plan; Schinkel never designed a pedestal more elegant than the travertine base that supported Mies's Pavilion; and Wright never composed a more

*17. Sculpture court of Barcelona Pavilion with statue by Georg Kolbe.
(Courtesy, Mies van der Rohe)*

modern, more striking sweep of horizontals than those that gave the
Barcelona Pavilion its magnificent verve.

At one end of the Pavilion the green Tinian marble walls that
enclosed the interior seemed to slide out, under, and beyond the
roof-plane to form an enclosed sculpture court whose floor was
largely taken up by another reflecting pool, also lined with black glass.
On a small base in this pool Mies placed a statue by Georg Kolbe, and
the resulting composition has become a favourite example of those
who advocate collaboration between architects on the one hand, and
sculptors and painters on the other [17]. The Kolbe did, indeed, look
beautiful in this setting; but while Mies always intended to put a
figure into this little court, the idea that he collaborated with Kolbe
in the design of this setting is, unfortunately, a myth. The truth is that
Mies was very anxious to borrow a Lehmbruck figure for this spot;
and when this proved to be impossible to arrange, he grabbed a taxi
on one of his last days in Berlin before leaving for Barcelona, drove
out to Kolbe's studio, and borrowed the best substitute he could find.
... Although the success of the Kolbe in this classic court does not
prove that collaboration between artists and architects is unnecessary,
it does suggest that there may be other and better ways towards integration of the arts.

18. *Interior of Barcelona Pavilion with 'Barcelona' chairs and stools.*
(*Courtesy, Mies van der Rohe*)

In addition to the Kolbe statue, there were only about a dozen objects exhibited in the Barcelona Pavilion – and all were exquisite. Specifically, the exhibit consisted of a couple of Mies's so-called Barcelona chairs, half a dozen Barcelona stools of related design [18], and two or three glass-topped tables also generally related to the chairs in concept. That concept was to take two modified X shapes of flat, chromium-plated steel bars, join them with crossbars in two or three places, apply to them a web of broad leather straps, and rest leather-covered pillows on the webbing to form the actual seating surfaces [19]. In the case of the tables, the modified X frame was topped by inch-thick slabs of glass.

The delicate curvature of the X-shaped legs, the perfect finish of the plated steel and the leather upholstery, and the magnificent, almost monumental proportions of the pieces – all these factors have made Mies's Barcelona furniture 'timeless', rather than easily dated. Like everything else Mies did at Barcelona, these pieces were expensive to make; but they were made to last through the ages, both in terms of solidity and in terms of design.

Unfortunately, the Barcelona Pavilion was dismantled at the close of the exhibition and shipped back to Germany in pieces. Where it ended up, Mies was never able to discover. Yet its influence upon modern architects the world over has been tremendous. Some of Wright's best Usonian houses of the late 1930s were quite clearly influenced by the grandiose simplicity of the Barcelona Pavilion – just as Mies had been influenced by the sweep of Wright's Robie house of 1908. But quite apart from Wright (who, needless to say, never acknowledged any such influences), there were and are numerous others – especially among the younger generation of modern architects – who are unable to this day to escape the powerful impact of this jewel-like structure. Most of Paul Rudolph's early houses in Florida, in the late 1940s and early 1950s, were variations on the Barcelona theme; I. M. Pei's penthouse office for William Zeckendorf, on a roof-top above Madison Avenue, is in part almost a replica of the 1929 Pavilion – as are some of the beautiful details of the plaza at the base of Pei's Mile High Center in Denver, Colorado. In Los Angeles, of course, a highly successful firm of architects built a near-copy of the Barcelona Pavilion out of stucco and sheet aluminium and turned it into the firm's offices. From Tokyo to Stockholm the Barcelona Pavilion has been copied in large or small part, in cheap or precious materials, again and again. And the monumental Mies-sized chairs and tables designed for Barcelona remain to this day the only standard modern pieces the leading architects of the U.S. and Europe find suitable for the furnishing of important spaces in public buildings. Indeed, the reception-room in the offices of Skidmore, Owings & Merrill, in New York – a firm that has designed and built more 'Miesian' buildings than Mies himself – is furnished entirely with Mies's Barcelona chairs, and lined with the same glass walls set in chromium which Mies developed for Barcelona! Finally, in 1962, a group of West German architects decided that a replica of the Barcelona Pavilion should be erected as a small monument in a park – possibly in Mies's home town of Aachen. If the funds for the undertaking can be found, the Pavilion may be preserved for posterity.

Mies's critics have pointed out, with some justification, that he is at his best when there are no serious functional problems to solve and when there are no budget limitations worth mentioning. They have said that Mies is really an architectural sculptor – admittedly a master at the manipulation of spaces and forms, materials and finishes – but that architecture is a mixture in equal parts of function and aesthetics. Mies's answer to this is that buildings have a long life; that most of them outlive their original function and must adapt themselves to different uses; and that the only permanent ingredient a building can be expected to possess is beauty. History, of course, is on Mies's side; nobody remembers whether the Parthenon ever worked really well, but everyone remembers what Phidias did there for the eternal splendour and glory of architecture. By the same token, no one will long remember that the German Pavilion at Barcelona contained no exhibits – and could not have contained many exhibits – in the conventional sense; but history will record that in 1929, on a hill above Barcelona, Mies van der Rohe built the most beautiful structure of an era.

19. 'Barcelona' chair, 1929. (Courtesy, Museum of Modern Art)

EIGHT

The Barcelona Pavilion was no isolated flash in the pan. During the two or three years after the Pavilion was dismantled, Mies produced half a dozen houses, stores, and exhibits of similar simplicity, precision, and clarity. The best of these designs were two residences: the Tugendhat house in Brno, Czechoslovakia, built in 1930; and the exhibition house for the Berlin Building exhibition of 1931.

What the Villa Savoye is in Le Corbusier's career, what the Robie house is in Wright's work, the Tugendhat house is in Mies's development. In fact, it would be possible to tell the broad story of modern architecture in terms of these three houses – Savoye, Robie, and Tugendhat. It is difficult to imagine that many of today's modern houses would look the way they do without the prior creation of these three.

Although the Tugendhat house was actually a very practical affair full of closed-off bedrooms, dressing-rooms, kitchens, pantries, and all the other 'functional' areas that are supposed to give Mies so much trouble, it will be remembered best for its magnificent living space – a huge, open area, walled on three sides with glass extending from floor to ceiling, and subdivided into four or five different and smaller spaces by the merest suggestion of a screen or a free-standing cabinet (today's 'space-divider') [20]. To all intents and purposes, the Tugendhat house was the first 'glass house' – the first of a whole series of spacious and airy constructions that allowed the trees and lawns to form the visual boundaries of the interior. In many ways the Tugendhat house was very similar to the Barcelona Pavilion in its extraordinarily open plan and its completely free flow of space – much freer than anything ever attempted by Wright up to that time.

Like the Barcelona Pavilion, the Tugendhat house had cross- rather than H-shaped chromium-plated steel columns, spaced far apart to support the roof-slab; like the Pavilion, it had free-standing walls of the most precious materials available to the architect – gold and white onyx for some walls, striped black and brown Macassar

20. Living area in Tugendhat house, Brno, Czechoslovakia, 1930. Study is at left. (Courtesy, Mies van der Rohe)

21. Tugendhat dining area, screened by a semi-circular wall of ebony. Only the 'functional' ceiling lights seem dated in retrospect. (Courtesy, Museum of Modern Art)

22. *Living-room at night, Tugendhat house. The chairs were specially designed for this house.* (*Courtesy, Mies van der Rohe*)

ebony for a truly majestic semi-circular screen around the dining area [21], black and beige shantung for the curtains. The floors of the Tugendhat house were of white linoleum.

Into this most elegant setting, Mies carefully placed several of his Barcelona chairs and stools, together with a series of new chairs and tables just as beautiful as those he had designed for Barcelona. The finest piece – another classic still in common use today – was a glass-topped coffee table supported on a cross of flat, chromium-plated steel bars [22]. As in every one of his designs, from skyscrapers to dining-chairs, Mies reduced each object to its essential elements, and then refined each detail to a point of almost breathtaking beauty and eloquence. There was nothing in this house which did not reflect this process of distillation to the point of utter perfection – not a window mullion, not a heating pipe, not a lighting fixture, not an ash-tray. The Barcelona chairs and the special Tugendhat chairs designed by Mies – an upholstered version of the cantilever-chair

23. The cantilever principle applied to an easy chair. Mies designed it for use in the Tugendhat house, in 1929. (Courtesy, Museum of Modern Art)

principle patented by him [23] – were covered with natural pigskin or white vellum; a square rug of natural wool formed an 'island' in the open space, defining the main living area; and a Lehmbruck bust on a square pedestal formed the focal point of that space.

No wonder Gropius is supposed to have said, when seeing this villa, that it was a 'Sunday house'. It is difficult to imagine the place overrun by hordes of happy, mud-caked children. Yet this is almost what happened after the Second World War, when the local Czech authorities turned the empty and somewhat damaged Tugendhat house into a gymnasium – with parallel bars along the walls – and painted the white linoleum a bright red. A visiting American student was able to take a snapshot of the house, which she showed to Mies. 'And you know,' Mies said later, with a grin, 'it didn't look bad at all!'

In its prime, the Tugendhat house made several points about architecture in a masterly way. Its site was difficult, as the land sloped abruptly and the entrance had to be on the uphill side. Mies treated the top or entrance floor somewhat like a Corbu roof-garden, with curved and rectangular forms making a free and open composition. However, one of the most difficult aspects of siting a building on a steep slope is not the question of entrance levels, but the question of how to treat the *sides* of the building. Most architects simply let the natural slope of the land continue past the short sides of their structure, hoping that no one will catch a side-view of what looks like a building taking a toboggan ride downhill. Mies, who never leaves a detail to chance (for 'God is in the details'), cut back into the slope and framed the Tugendhat house between two level courts carved out of the hillside. As a result, the house looks solidly anchored in the hill, surrounded by terraces that dramatize the natural slope and make the hill 'architectural'. (This sort of thing would, of course, be frowned upon by Wright's followers, but Mies felt – with Corbu – that if you are an architect, you might as well treat your site architecturally rather than let the site swallow you up in its own untrammelled contours.)

The Tugendhat house showed Mies intensely sensitive to colour. Actually, there were no real *colours* in the house at all – only the muted, natural tones of marble, wood, silk, and leather. Mies's palette is just about confined to whites and off-whites, and blacks and off-blacks. There are never any bright colour accents as there are in Corbu's work. One reason for this is that in the glass houses Mies developed since Tugendhat, the ever-changing colours in nature are a major part of the spatial experience indoors. 'When you have a white house with glass walls,' Mies said some years later about his Farnsworth house near Chicago, 'you see the trees and bushes and the sky framed in white – and the white emphasizes all the beautiful colours in the landscape.' So, in the Tugendhat house, Mies made the landscape his 'wallpaper'; indeed, one of the glass walls was really a glass case, filled with planting that lent touches of colour to the interior in every season.

Those who denounce Mies as 'cold' and call for a more 'romantic' approach have completely failed to see how he has used the resources of nature – of the trees and the sun – to make his architecture vibrant with life and colour. From the outside, his glass walls reflect the changing seasons, the drifting clouds, the colours of sky and leaves. In the glass skyscrapers, Mies had taken a leaf from Wright's book: he had made each glass wall a many-faceted diamond whose every face would reflect a different sort of scene. The result was a mosaic of refractions and reflections, for each sheet of glass was set into its frame at an angle slightly different from that of the adjoining sheets, so that each sheet tended to reflect a slightly different image. In a house, Mies felt, such a system would produce too many window divisions, and these would obstruct the view from the inside out. The view *out* of a glass *house* is just as important as its exterior appearance [24]; for the landscape suddenly becomes the space within which you live, and the building itself dissolves in its natural setting. The view *out* of a glass *office building*, on the other hand, is less important, and here Mies felt that closely spaced window divisions could be justified. On an urban or suburban site, a house with unshielded glass walls obviously makes no sense, and Mies designed a whole series of beautiful court or patio houses, with walled-in gardens, to cope with the problem of privacy combined with the need for spaciousness presented by just such sites. These court houses are, in reality, a single space; part of it

24. *Tugendhat living-room. Glass walls at right could be lowered into a pocket built into the floor. Glass wall at end of room is really a small greenhouse, containing year-round planting. (Courtesy, Mies van der Rohe)*

is roofed over and faced with glass where it looks out over the rest of the court; the balance is a walled garden, and each interior space partakes of that garden. Between 1931 and 1938 Mies designed and built several such court houses, and projected others in his airy and brilliant sketches. These projects remain a prime source of inspiration to many architects building in crowded suburban areas.

Despite the colourful and ever-changing reflections and views of nature made possible by Mies's glass buildings, it is obvious that he always shied away from bright colours and brilliant contrasts of light and dark. He was and is, after all, the man of eternal understatement, and bright colours and bright sunshine have no appeal to Mies's reserve. 'I remember the first time I ever went to Italy,' Mies recalled recently. 'The sun and the blue skies were so bright, I thought I'd go crazy! I couldn't wait to go back to the north, where everything was grey and subtle.' To somebody as preoccupied as Mies is with the extraction of the finest nuances from the simplest object, the brightness of the Mediterranean was nothing but sheer bombast. Even in commissioning photography of his American buildings, Mies has tried hard to get the same sort of grey, slightly grim, and very contrastless pictures of his buildings which he used to be able to get in Germany in the 1920s.

The year after Tugendhat was completed, Mies built another sort of house – a full-sized dwelling unit shown in the great hall of the Berlin Building exhibition. This house was all on one level; its plan presupposed a relatively small site, so that most of the glass walls faced a court or patio surrounded by garden walls [25]. This was a very practical house, by Mies's standards, zoned for different kinds of activity, yet extremely open in plan. Like the Tugendhat house and the Barcelona Pavilion (which it resembled in plan), its rooms were modulated and defined only by free-standing walls that overlapped and produced compositions of planes and volumes which, in turn, allowed all interior spaces to merge with the surrounding gardens. The roof was again supported on a few columns – in this case, pipe columns that had been chromium-plated like those in the earlier structures [26]. (The chromium-plating, incidentally, turned the column surfaces into reflecting mirrors that tended to make the columns seem much more slender than they actually were.) All furniture was, as usual, by Mies, and it included some beautifully detailed storage walls and the by then standard assortment of cantilever and Barcelona chairs and tables. Although the finishes employed here were not as precious as those

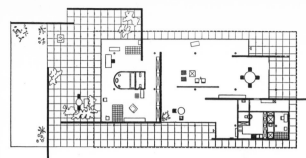

25. Plan of the model house for the Berlin exhibition. The plan is an adaptation of that of the Barcelona Pavilion to the special needs of a residence. (Courtesy, Museum of Modern Art)

used at Barcelona and Tugendhat, the white-walled exhibition house had a tremendously elegant and costly look. At the same exhibition Mies also showed a 'bachelor's apartment' consisting of a single space divided, by various means, into sleeping, living, and dining areas. Here, as in the exhibition house, Mies incorporated some of the finest contemporary paintings and sculpture in the architectural setting. And here, as in all his work since Barcelona, Mies showed a calm mastery of detail and of total composition which made his work the most self-assured architecture then being created in Europe.

26. Living-room in house for the Berlin Building exhibition, 1931. Pipe columns were chromium-plated. (Courtesy, Museum of Modern Art)

In 1930 Mies was appointed Director of the Bauhaus in Dessau. The Bauhaus had been Gropius's great experiment; he had taken over the school at the end of the First World War, when it was located in Weimar. An arts-and-crafts school originally, the Bauhaus had been founded in 1902 and had been directed prior to the war by the great Belgian architect Henry van de Velde. Gropius turned it into the first serious laboratory for the development of an *industrial* art. 'Art and technology – the new unity' had become the Bauhaus slogan; and the work done at the Bauhaus, under Gropius, completely transformed product design in Europe in less than a decade. Some of the finest architects, designers, and painters had been brought together by him to run the school: men like the architect Marcel Breuer, the designers Herbert Bayer, Joseph Albers, and L. Moholy-Nagy, and the painters Paul Klee, Wassily Kandinsky, and Lyonel Feininger had helped him make the Bauhaus the outstanding centre of modern architecture and modern design of its time in the world.

By 1926 the Bauhaus had grown to the point where new quarters were required, and Gropius moved the school from Weimar to Dessau. There he built one of the most extraordinary complexes of buildings to be erected anywhere in the 1920s. The principal element of this dynamic complex was a structure sheathed entirely in glass. It was a logical extension of the two glass-and-steel structures Gropius built before the First World War, and quite similar in concept to Mies's proposal for a glass 'curtain wall' to be draped over the 'bones' of his two skyscrapers.

The Bauhaus was beset by problems from the start. This was, of course, unavoidable in any effort based on as radical a concept as that proposed by Gropius. Some of the difficulties arose from philosophical conflicts: the early days of the Bauhaus were strongly influenced by German Expressionists and their arts-and-crafts romanticism. Other difficulties were political: although Gropius was determined to stick to the central issues he himself had outlined for the school, there were political pressures from the extreme Left inside the Bauhaus, and the extreme Right outside the Bauhaus. Still, all went reasonably well until February 1928, when Gropius decided that it was best for him and the Bauhaus if he resigned his post as Director. There followed a more or less chaotic period during which, at one time, a group of Communists dominated the direction of the school; until finally the Dessau authorities (the Bauhaus was a public institution) decided to make a clean sweep of it and put the Bauhaus back in order. They asked Gropius for his recommendations of a man to serve as Director, and Gropius suggested Mies.

One of the first things that happened to Mies when he took over at Dessau was that he was faced with a minor scandal. A woman instructor was involved, and there was to be an investigation. Mies, who had not the slightest idea of what was going on, called up Kandinsky and asked him if he would come along to the hearing to help out. 'Kandinsky, who was trained as a lawyer, said he'd be delighted,' Mies recalls. 'He thought it might be fun!' Next, Mies telephoned Paul Klee with the same request. 'Klee said that he'd rather go to see a dentist than listen to this sort of mess,' Mies continued. 'That's when I really began to like Klee.'

The next thing that happened to the new Director was that a student delegation appeared to inform him that there would be a student strike unless certain demands were met immediately. Mies looked at the delegates coldly, and said: 'You are here to work and learn. Anyone not present at his classes in the morning will be expelled.' Within a remarkably short time the Bauhaus had stopped being a circus for Bohemian radicals and had gone back to being a workshop.

Still, political developments in Germany and, more particularly, in the Province of Anhalt (in which Dessau was located) began to endanger the Bauhaus. By 1932 Anhalt was dominated by a Nazi governor and a Nazi legislature, and the Bauhaus was forced to move to Berlin. Mies rented an empty factory and set up the school inside it. 'We just painted it all white inside,' he recalls. 'It looked fine.' But the situation was getting to be increasingly difficult in Berlin as well. In January 1933 Hitler came to power, and the Bauhaus was again under attack. The Nazis not only objected to the Bauhaus because it had once been briefly identified with Communist influences; they objected to its sort of design and to its sort of architecture, which they considered 'Bolshevist' and 'degenerate', as well as 'un-German'.

Mies and a few collaborators tried to hold the fort, but by the autumn of 1933 the situation had become virtually hopeless. Mies arranged an interview with one of the Nazis' 'cultural experts', Alfred Rosenberg, and they met late one night in Rosenberg's office.

We talked for an hour or more [Mies has said]. It was quite a peaceful discussion. Rosenberg told me: 'If only you would drop the name Bauhaus, then we might be able to work things out.' I said: 'But that is a wonderful name – Bauhaus [House of Building] – in fact, it's almost the best thing about the school!' Finally, Rosenberg agreed to let us continue.

Mies left the Nazi leader's office and went across the street to a restaurant where some of his close associates had been waiting anxiously, afraid that he might be arrested for having had the nerve to stand up and talk back to a Nazi boss. Lilly Reich, the brilliant furniture designer who had collaborated with Mies on some of the exhibitions in the 1920s, was among those waiting for him. Mies reported on his interview with Rosenberg, and everyone was elated. There were drinks all around. Then Mies said, quietly: 'I have something to tell you. Now that they have agreed to let us continue, *we* are going to close the Bauhaus! I have written out a statement saying that the Bauhaus cannot continue to exist in this atmosphere.' There was shock and deep consternation, but Mies prevailed. The Bauhaus, in its original form, was closed for ever.

Mies stayed on in Germany for another three or four years. He was able to build a few smaller houses (though to do a modern house was becoming increasingly difficult in the face of Nazi pressures to force all architecture into neo-classicism or romanticism), and he had time to develop several beautiful projects for court and terrace houses. Many of these projects never went beyond the stage of eloquent sketches, but even these sketches have served to inspire a whole new generation of young architects in the U.S. and elsewhere. There were also two projects for office buildings. The first was an entry in a competition for the headquarters of the Reichsbank in Berlin; it was rejected in favour of other designs more in conformity with the Nazi party line in architecture. The second, an administrative centre for the German silk industry, was – like the Reichsbank building – symmetrical, monumental in scale, but entirely rational in expression. Neither of these two office structures was ever built.

In the spring of 1937 the American architect Philip C. Johnson, who had long been an ardent admirer of Mies, suggested to Mr and Mrs Stanley Resor (of the J. Walter Thompson Advertising Agency) that they should engage Mies to design for them a country house on a spectacular site in Jackson Hole, Wyoming. Johnson had had several earlier contacts with Mies: he had visited Germany on a number of occasions and met Mies when the latter was Director of the Bauhaus. Together with the critic and historian Henry-Russell Hitchcock, Johnson had, in 1932, arranged the Museum of Modern Art's exhibition of 'International Architecture' and published the famous accompanying catalogue – a book in which the term 'International Style' made its first public appearance. Mies's work was, of course, included in the Modern Museum exhibition, as were photographs and models of buildings by Frank Lloyd Wright, Le Corbusier, Gropius, and others. In short, Mies was quite well known to the American avant-garde by the time the invitation came from the Resors to visit America.

Mies arrived there in the summer of 1937, and went out to Wyoming to study the site. (Though the Resor house was never built, Mies's studies for it are as clear a demonstration as he ever made of the importance of the landscape in glass architecture [27].) On one of his trips through Chicago he met the architect John Holabird, who was then looking for a man to head the School of Architecture at Chicago's Armour Institute (later to be known as the Illinois Institute of Technology). Holabird thought that Mies was exactly the man for the job, and asked him what his terms were. 'A completely free hand, and $10,000 a year,' Mies answered. Holabird telephoned President Heald of Armour, then turned to Mies and said: 'You can have a free hand, but they can't quite afford the salary.' Mies accepted none

27. Resor house project for Jackson Hole, Wyoming, 1938. Because the landscape is all-important in a glass house, architectural elements were underplayed to emphasize the view. (Courtesy, Mies van der Rohe)

the less and in 1938 moved to Chicago for good to become the Director of Architecture at Heald's Institute. Twenty years later, when the age-limits of the Illinois Institute of Technology (I.I.T.) finally forced Mies to retire, he had set up one of the most impressive – and unusual – Schools of Architecture in the world, and trained some of the best men now heading the staffs of American architectural offices. I.I.T., for its part, had given Mies the chance to design its entire campus (and build a large part of it), and to construct also some of the faculty and student housing along the perimeter of the campus. I.I.T. also had, by the time Mies retired, managed to raise his salary to the amount he had originally requested.

'Ladies and gentlemen,' Frank Lloyd Wright said, his arm across Mies's shoulders, 'I give you Mies van der Rohe. But for me, there would have been no Mies . . . I admire him as an architect and respect and love him as a man. Armour Institute, *I* give you *my* Mies van der Rohe. You treat him well and love him as I do.' With that, Wright stepped down off the platform and walked out.

The occasion was a dinner in the ballroom of Chicago's Palmer House, given to present the new Director of Architecture to the faculty and trustees of Armour. Mies had asked Wright to introduce him, and Wright did it in his own, inimitable style. Mies's English, in those days, was practically nonexistent (it later became quite fluent, if a little rough), and he replied in German with a speech that must have taken him a year or more to write – or, to be exact, a lifetime. But before he started out on his prepared speech, Mies paid an eloquent and extemporaneous tribute to Wright. Although no record remains of that tribute, Mies did, a couple of years later, write an appreciation for the Museum of Modern Art's catalogue to its 1940 Wright exhibition. The catalogue was never published because disagreements arose between Wright and the Museum regarding some of its contents, but Mies's tribute to Wright is on record. 'In his undiminishing power,' Mies wrote, 'Wright resembles a giant tree in a wide landscape which, year after year, attains a more noble crown.' Mies is so painfully modest about certain aspects of his own work that he never seriously objected to Wright's bombastic assumptions of fatherhood for the entire modern movement. In later years, after the Second World War, Mies was hurt by Wright's intemperate attacks upon him and the International Style in general, but never ceased to admire Wright's own work.

What Mies had to say in his inaugural address at Armour was, in a sense, completely autobiographical. It is worth quoting almost in full, for, in these aphorisms, Mies told not only the story of his own life and work, but laid down the law to Armour Institute's students of architecture and established a code of discipline and of morality which will live long after Mies is gone.

True education is concerned not only with practical goals but also with values [Mies began]. Our aims assure us of our material life; our values make possible our spiritual life. In its simplest form, architecture is rooted in entirely functional considerations, but it can reach up through all degrees of value to the highest sphere of spiritual existence, into the realm of pure art.

In organizing a system for architectural education we must recognize this situation if we are to succeed . . . We must fit the system to this reality. Any teaching of architecture must explain these relations and interrelations. *We must make clear, step by step, what things are possible, necessary and significant.*

If teaching has any purpose, it is to implant true insight and responsibility. Education must lead us from irresponsible opinion to true responsible judgement. It must lead us from chance and arbitrariness to rational clarity and intellectual order. Therefore let us guide our students over the road of discipline from materials, through function, to creative work.

Let us lead them into the healthy world of primitive building methods, where there was meaning in every stroke of an axe, expression in every bite of a chisel. Where can we find greater structural clarity than in the wooden buildings of old? Where else can we find such unity of material, construction and form? Here the wisdom of whole generations is stored.

What feelings for material and what power of expression there is in these buildings! What warmth and beauty they have! They seem to be echoes of old songs.

Mies went on to describe, with unexpected passion, the quality of stone and brick, their texture, pattern, bonding, the richness of their colour. Several years later, when Nikolaus Pevsner, the art historian and an editor of the *Architectural Review*, wrote to architectural schools throughout the world to discover what methods they used in teaching design, Mies answered for I.I.T. by saying that he first taught his students how to build with wood, then with stone, then with brick, and, finally, with concrete and with steel. By that time, Mies continued, the students were just about ready to graduate from I.I.T.; and after a few years of additional, practical experience, some of them might be expected to become designers! Pevsner, who thought that Mies had misunderstood the question, wrote again, but Mies simply explained the system in additional detail. If such an educational programme seems only reasonable to the layman (who assumes that one must learn to walk before one learns to run), it should be explained that most modern architectural schools take a very different view: they believe that it is quite proper for students to be designing sky-scrapers long before they have been taught anything about the steel or concrete structure or the lift systems without which skyscrapers cannot work. Only at Mies's I.I.T. and at Wright's Taliesin did students first learn the fundamentals of building before they were permitted even to think about problems of design.

Mies made this point clear in his inaugural address when he came to speak of modern materials. 'Each material has its specific character-istics which we must understand if we want to use it,' Mies said. In other words, no design is possible until the materials with which you design are completely understood.

This is no less true of steel and concrete [than of wood, brick, and stone]. We must remember that everything depends on how we use a material, not on the material itself . . . New materials are not necessarily superior. *Each material is only what we make it.*

We must be as familiar with the functions of our building as with our materials [Mies continued]. We must learn what a building can be, what it should be, *and also what it must not be* . . . And just as we acquaint our-selves with materials, just as we must understand functions, so we must become familiar with the psychological and spiritual factors of our day. No cultural activity is possible otherwise; for we are dependent on the spirit of our time.

What did Mies mean by the 'spirit of our time'? He explained by saying that 'at this point, the problem of technology arises . . . Technology not only promises greatness and power, but also involves dangers; good and evil apply to it as they do to all human actions; it is our task to make the right decision.' And then, in a precise and characteristic sentence, Mies said: '*Every decision leads to a special kind of order.*'

The decisions Mies referred to have to do with emphasis. Is archi-tecture to be based primarily upon the material and functional require-ments of the day? No, Mies said. 'Means must be subsidiary to ends and to our desire for dignity and value.' What about some idealistic principle of order as a basis for our architecture? Again Mies said no; such ideal systems of order overemphasize form and have nothing to do with simple reality or our sense of what is practical. What, then, is the alternative?

We shall emphasize the *organic principle of order* as a means of achieving the successful relationship of the parts to each other and to the whole . . .

The long path from material through function to creative work has only one goal: to create order out of the desperate confusion of our time. We must have order, allocating to each thing its proper place and giving to each thing its due according to its nature. And here [Mies concluded] we shall take our stand.

Material, function, creative work – here 'we shall take our stand!' This rational progression, as stern a discipline as was ever developed by a religious order, has not only been the foundation of Mies's own work, but the foundation of Mies's school at I.I.T. as well. The students who soon came under his influence had to reconcile themselves to living a serious life of simple dedication: each had to measure up to the precise standards of draughtsmanship and of structural knowledge which Mies had once trained himself to meet; or else they had to go on to a less single-minded school. In the circumstances, it is not surprising that a kind of hero worship of Mies soon sprang up at I.I.T. – a development that Mies, unconsciously, helped to cultivate by his extreme reticence and shyness in public. Mies brought with him a number of old associates, including the architect and city planner Ludwig Hilberseimer, who had built one of the Weissenhof structures in Stuttgart ten years earlier. Some of his associates have tended to surround Mies with the aura due to an *éminence grise* and excessively to protect him from the outside world. When strangers are finally brought into Mies's presence, they are often surprised to find a simple, friendly, unpretentious man who loves to reminisce over a few drinks after dinner, and whose pleasures – in addition to living and breathing architecture, reading the works of German philosophers, and looking at his beautiful collection of Klee paintings – are largely confined to puffing away at huge cigars.

Mies's own mode of living in Chicago contributed quite a bit to the aura of mystery which has surrounded him ever since his arrival in the U.S. He inhabits a spacious apartment in an old building a block away from Lake Michigan. He generally lives there alone, though one of his three daughters, an art historian, used to share the apartment with him. (Another daughter, now back in Germany, is a successful actress in Munich. Mies's marriage to their mother ended in divorce in the early 1930s.)

On the surface, Mies lives much like any other quiet, sometimes lonely, elderly gentleman. Yet his apartment is anything but typical, for it has remained, to all intents and purposes, quite unfurnished ever since Mies moved into it. Except for the living-room, which contains several well-proportioned, black-upholstered settees and easy chairs of square silhouette, the apartment has almost no furniture at all. Its only décor is Mies's magnificent collection of Klees, carefully hung on white and otherwise empty walls, and just as carefully lit. An occasional marble shelf completes the 'decorative scheme'.

Mies lives in this monastic setting according to a rather peculiar schedule established by himself and respected by his friends and associates. As he rarely talks until after dinner (when, in the right sort of atmosphere, he may become very voluble and cheerful), he does not go to bed until the early hours of the morning, and does not rise until fairly late the next day. No one who values Mies's friendship would telephone him before 11 a.m., at which time he may, under extreme duress, produce a few pleasant and thoughtful grunts. By the time lunch is over, he may feel inclined to become a little more articulate; in his office he is likely to sit and examine a scale model of one of his latest buildings, asking an assistant to shift walls around very slightly – or back again just as slightly. (This process may consume several weeks or months; the 'simpler' the building looks, the longer it is likely to take.) During these sessions with scale models of buildings and full-size mock-ups of building parts (all the walls in Mies's buildings are studied in precise, full-size mock-ups prepared in a model workshop that is as well equipped as any jeweller's), Mies may communicate with others by an occasional smile between puffs at his ever-present cigar. There are not likely to be very many spoken words, and the atmosphere tends to be that of an operating room while a great surgeon is preparing to perform a revolutionary operation for the first time.

Mies was able to establish his own private architectural practice in Chicago shortly after taking over the position at Armour Institute; for the President of Armour, Dr Henry Heald (later to become President of the Ford Foundation), decided to entrust the planning and design of the entire new I.I.T. campus to him. Mies's designs for the campus covering eight city blocks were so radically different from anything he had attempted before – and so convincing in terms of American building technology – that the I.I.T. buildings are now among the most influential works of architecture ever produced in the U.S. [28–32].

This is doubly astonishing, for when Mies attempted I.I.T., he was more than fifty years old and could easily have been expected to concentrate on a further development of his European work; conversely, he could hardly have been expected to see the nature of modern

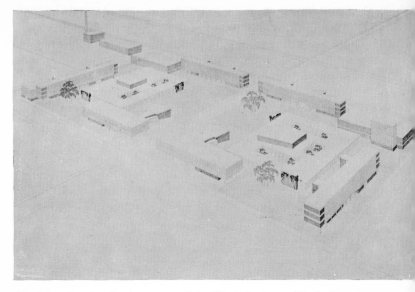

28. Original project for the campus of the Illinois Institute of Technology, Chicago, 1939. (Courtesy, Mies van der Rohe)

American building technology with as much clarity as he did – for, after all, he was only a newcomer. Yet the I.I.T. buildings are so simple, so obvious, so entirely reasonable in structure and structural expression, that it remains a major mystery why no one else had put up these buildings long before Mies arrived in Chicago!

Gordon Bunshaft, Mies's admirer and the designer of Lever House, has said that 'America is largely a steel-building country'. Mies saw this clearly as soon as he arrived in Chicago, and proceeded to draw the logical conclusions: a skeleton of steel becomes a simple cage, with columns and beams set at regular intervals. Such a cage may be filled with many different materials: brick, glass, concrete, or what have you. Once Mies understood the nature of the steel cage, it seemed to him that brick and glass were the obvious, economical, and natural complements of steel. Brick is small in scale, easily handled, easily fitted around the flanges of steel columns and beams, easily recognized for its familiar size – a fact that immediately gives any onlooker a true sense of the scale and the dimensions of the building before him. Glass, set into steel or aluminium frames, could be attached with similar ease to the flanges of a steel cage and could be given a proper scale by divisions into window-panes of different (or identical) sizes. And because glass is transparent, it clearly reveals the structural cage. The obvious solution for a modern industrial enclosure, therefore, was a straightforward grid of steel filled in with brick and glass.

Material – function – creative work. Mies had found the right materials. What about the function? Here Mies developed a concept so radical within the modern movement that it is still being fought by many of his contemporaries. Louis Sullivan had said that 'form follows function' – or, at least, Sullivan's partner, Dankmar Adler, had said it, and Sullivan had accepted the idea with a grain or two of salt. But Mies decided to find out whether this was really a valid maxim. Did not buildings tend to outlive their original functions? Did not functions change with increasing frequency in the modern world? Was it really possible to predict, in 1940, what functions the laboratories and machine shops and classroom structures at I.I.T. might be called upon to fulfil in 1950 or 1960 or in the year 2000? Obviously not, Mies decided. The only function one could be sure of in any building built to last was *the function of flexibility of use throughout its lifetime*. So, the only kind of building which would make sense, in terms of functionalism, would be a building not adjusted to any specific function at all!

This conception of the 'universal building' probably came to Mies out of his knowledge of Schinkel and the classical tradition. For the greatest contribution the classicists had made to our civilization – from the Parthenon to the Greek Revival – was the idea of universality. They believed that mankind needed not *special* but *universal* solutions – solutions as applicable to a temple as they might be to a palace, as reasonable in a museum as in a customs house. What Mies did at I.I.T. was to take the classical notion of universality and translate it into steel, brick, and glass. I.I.T. – a campus dedicated to research into the wide world of ever-changing sciences – became a collection of beautifully detailed standard units, based upon an identical module, and designed to be so flexible as to be capable of accommodating almost any kind of activity in the years to come.

How radical a notion this was for the U.S. in particular is not always clearly understood. An American businessman, to whom one of Mies's friends explained this notion of universality, was horror-struck! 'Do you realize what this means?' he asked. 'Don't you know that the entire economic system of the U.S. is based upon the rapid obsolescence of our buildings, cars, consumer goods? If buildings were designed with so much flexibility that they would never wear out – well, that would wreck our whole building industry!' This shortsighted point of view formed the real basis of many hysterical attacks upon Mies during the years immediately after the Second World War; only in the late 1950s, as it became evident that even the U.S. would have trouble in providing the amount and variety of shelter needed by an exploding population, did Mies's earlier critics begin to understand how much sense his 'universal space' concept would make on a globe populated by three billion people or more.

Material and function were solved at I.I.T. with Mies's characteristic clarity and simplicity. What about 'creative work'? One Chicago architect, looking at the first I.I.T. buildings, said that they looked to him like little more than warehouses thrown up by some contractor. He was absolutely right, though not in the way he meant it. For the 'little more' – the 'little' difference – made *all* the difference. Marcel Breuer once listed all the ingredients that went into the design of his buildings, and ended up with 'that intangible one per cent which is art'. Mies might raise that to ten per cent or even thirty-three per cent, but he would agree that, regardless of the percentage, the quality that is art is intangible and elusive. Yet it is much less so in Mies's work than it is in the work of Wright or Le Corbusier. 'What makes Mies such a great influence,' Philip Johnson once said, 'is that he is so easy to copy.' There are plenty of Miesian buildings that tend to disprove this dictum; but the fact is that Mies has always been able to reduce his ideas and methods to a precision unequalled in our time. At I.I.T. the intangible, unifying force 'which is art' is the repeated use of a standard unit, a structural bay twenty-four feet wide, twenty-four feet deep, and twelve feet high. This structural bay appears on most façades as a steel-framed rectangle twenty-four feet long and twelve feet high, i.e., a double square, one of the oldest and most effective proportional systems in architecture. This double square may be filled with brick or glass (or a combination of the two); but its dimensions are constant. Behind this rectangular façade system, there may be a variety of spaces: open workshops, classrooms, research laboratories, or what have you. But the universal façade embraces them all.

The second intangible quality that makes I.I.T. a 'little more' than a collection of warehouses is the quality of the spaces between the various rectangular buildings (most of them two or three storeys in height). Mies conceived the I.I.T. campus as a group of some twenty buildings forming a series of quadrangles; but, unlike the classical

29. *Typical court on I.I.T. campus. (Photo: Hedrich-Blessing)*

30. *Boiler plant at I.I.T., 1950. (Photo: Hedrich-Blessing)*

31. Chapel at I.I.T., 1952. (Photo: Hedrich-Blessing)

quadrangles of Oxford (or even of Harvard, with its gaps between buildings), Mies's quadrangles were a series of subtly interlocking spaces whose movement leads the visitor on from one court into the next, through a variety of spatial and formal experiences. This effect was achieved by making the planes and volumes of the individual buildings overlap in such a way that beyond each structure another one would become visible in the distance, 'sliding out' from behind the buildings in front of it and suggesting an unseen continuity of space beyond. Mies had achieved the same effect in his overlapping wall planes in the Barcelona Pavilion and in the Tugendhat house; here he was doing it on a grand, urban scale for the first time.

Mies's first building at I.I.T. was completed in 1943. Thirteen years and a dozen buildings later, Mies completed his part of the I.I.T. campus. His great friend, Dr Heald, had long before moved on to New York, and the new administration of the Institute decided, rather arbitrarily, that they wanted some other architects to try their hands

32. Faculty apartments at I.I.T., designed and built during the 1950s. These structures are of exposed concrete and brick. (Photo: Hedrich-Blessing)

at doing a building or two on the new campus. In 1958, therefore, I.I.T. approached Skidmore, Owings & Merrill, the big and highly skilled firm whose New York office was headed by Mies's friend, Bunshaft, and whose Chicago office was full of Mies's former students. Bunshaft, who was very disturbed by I.I.T.'s sudden rejection of Mies, suggested to him that he associate with the Chicago office and act as designer of the new building. Mies was rather touched and grateful, but told Bunshaft that he preferred not to 'come in through the back door. Anyway,' he added, 'the whole campus is already designed. Why not just carry it out?' Still, the gratuitous insult was unmistakable, and the I.I.T. student paper ran a front-page protest. Mies decided that he was much too busy to bother with the small minds now in charge of I.I.T. and that it was a waste of time to fight. In any event, the Skidmore, Owings & Merrill office was likely to produce something reasonably close to a Mies building; and it was also likely to respect Mies's site-plan concept. In short, the over-all harmony of the campus was not likely to be seriously affected. Still, in an age that has plenty of individual buildings – individual statements – by self-important, individual architects, and depressingly few unified *groups* of buildings, the opportunity missed at I.I.T. is likely to hurt architecture more than the powers-that-be may have realized.

The house that Mies designed for the Resors in Wyoming – and that was his immediate reason for coming to the U.S. – was never built. But shortly after the end of the Second World War, Mies began work on another house, which has probably had as great an influence on recent domestic architecture in America as any single work of the post-war years.

The client for this house was Dr Edith Farnsworth, a brilliant Chicago physician who had been a close friend of Mies for several years. In 1946 she bought a piece of land on the Fox River in Plano, Illinois, about an hour's ride from Chicago, and Mies began to design a house for her to be built on that site.

The Farnsworth house is, in all likelihood, the most complete statement of glass-and-steel, skin-and-bones architecture Mies or anyone else will ever be able to make [33]. It is also the ultimate in universality, the ultimate in precision and polish, the ultimate in the crystallization of an idea.

The house is a rectangular structure of eight steel columns, set in two parallel rows some twenty-eight feet apart. In the long direction of the plan the steel columns are spaced twenty-two feet apart. Between these eight columns there are held two slabs framed in steel – the floor and the roof. These slabs seem to float in the air (the floor-slab is about four feet above the ground, and the ceiling plane is about nine feet above that), and they are held between the steel H columns as if by some magnetic force. At each end the floor- and roof-slabs cantilever out six feet beyond the last row of columns.

Between these two floating slabs there is a simple glass-enclosed living space and porch. The living space is, to all intents and purposes, a single room, divided into sleeping, living, kitchen, and service areas. The floor throughout is of Italian travertine; the ceiling is white plaster; the few interior partitions are finished in natural primavera; the curtains inside the glass skin are of natural-coloured, off-white shantung; and the steel frame itself is painted white.

As a matter of fact, the steel frame was carefully polished before the coats of white paint were applied: first, all the welding marks at the connexions between columns and beams were ground down; next, Mies had the steel sand-blasted to get rid of the 'rough' texture of the rolled, structural sections; then he had a coat of zinc sprayed over the sand-blasted surface to prevent rust; and, finally, the white paint was applied with such care that the finished surfaces look almost baked on.

One reason for the elevation of the floor-plane above the grade is that the Fox River tends to rise and overflow its banks in the spring, so that the house looks like a pier or a boat during those days. Another reason is that Mies wanted a quality of airiness, of space-in-motion, which an earth-bound house would not have had to the same degree.

It took Mies six years to design and build this perfect jewel of a house. During this period his disciple, Philip Johnson, went ahead and built his own famous glass-and-steel house in New Canaan, Connecticut. Johnson has always made a point of saying that his house was designed *after* Mies had first developed the Farnsworth concept and that it was, therefore, based upon the Farnsworth house, although the latter was not completed until two years after Johnson moved into his own home. Actually, Johnson is unnecessarily modest in crediting Mies with all the qualities of his own house, for the Johnson and the Farnsworth houses – apart from being all steel and glass – are completely different in character. Johnson's house is symmetrical in its elevations; the Farnsworth house has a porch and a lower deck at one end and is quite dynamically asymmetrical. Johnson's house sits on the ground like a delightful little classical temple; the Farnsworth house is virtually airborne. Johnson's house has dark grey steel columns at all corners, containing the volume within the glass shell; the Farnsworth house has open corners and cantilevered ends, so that the interior space is projected outward into the landscape as in any structure by Wright. Finally, the Johnson house has a strong post-and-beam look, a feeling of compression in the columns; whereas the Farnsworth house has a sense of tension, of steel being stretched out to its ultimate potentials. (The white steel columns of the Farnsworth house are so precisely welded to the horizontal steel fascias of floor and roof planes that the steel 'sings' like a tuning-fork when it is lightly tapped.)

These differences between Johnson's and Mies's glass houses are

33. Farnsworth House, Plano, Illinois, 1950. View of entrance porches. Again the architecture is made to frame and reflect the surrounding landscape. (Photo: George H. Steuer)

more significant than they might seem. For what they add up to is this: Mies's house was a very 'American' sort of statement – dynamic, cantilevered, almost in motion; whereas Johnson (who was born in Ohio) had built a tiny, classical *palazzo* – a static, columnar, serene temple of a house. Mies's responsiveness to America – a continent of motion – began long before he came to Chicago; indeed, this quality of motion is already quite apparent in the Barcelona Pavilion (although the Pavilion *did* sit on a pedestal), and it is the quality Mies undoubtedly derived from Wright's Prairie houses.

Although the Farnsworth house was exquisitely simple and beautiful as an abstract statement about structure, skin, and space, it was hardly a 'house for family living'. Needless to say, it had never been intended to be that: it was meant to be a pleasure pavilion for a lady

85

living alone, and it was a perfect and expensive solution for that. Unfortunately, as the house neared completion, Mies's friendship with Dr Farnsworth broke up, and there was an extremely unpleasant aftermath, involving lawsuits (which were decided in Mies's favour), recriminations in public and private on the part of Dr Farnsworth, and denunciations of Mies as a menace to American architecture. This latter campaign, a rather ludicrous and silly bit of hysteria in retrospect (though it did hurt many of those involved), took the form of a concerted attack upon the International Style by the Hearst magazine *House Beautiful*.

In her April 1953 issue the editor of *House Beautiful* came forward with a ringing editorial denouncing the 'Threat to the New America'. The gist of the editorial was that a sinister group of International Stylists, led by Mies, Gropius, and Corbu, and supported by the Museum of Modern Art, was trying to force Americans to accept an architecture that was barren, grim, impoverished, impractical, uninhabitable, and destructive of individual possessions, as well as of individuals themselves. There was a hint or two that Communists were behind the whole thing. A list of International Style character- istics was published to warn readers of *House Beautiful* against the 'threat' – much in the same way that the F.B.I. warns the public against the 'ten most wanted' criminals of the day.

But the lady's principal ire was reserved for Mies's dictum: 'less is more'. This was the threat in a nutshell. 'We know that less is not more,' she wrote. 'It is simply less!' She was on pretty firm ground there, arithmetically speaking, though many of the great artists of all periods would have agreed with Mies on aesthetic grounds. For the purity of a miniature by Fra Angelico, say, is as much the result of a process of aesthetic distillation as is the Farns- worth house.

Although the attack was probably good for *House Beautiful*'s advertising and circulation, it was, perhaps, a little less good for some of the people most directly involved. Mies was shocked and unhappy. To him, the concept of universality in architecture implied the highest possible degree of freedom. For, after all, a building reduced to 'almost nothing' (Mies's phrase) represents the ultimate in non-interference on the part of an architect with the lives of his clients. To Mies, the architecture of 'nothingness' suggests a maxi- mum opportunity for free expression on the part of those who use the building: they can furnish it in any way they like, use it for anything they like, change its interior spaces in any manner that seems most suitable. If this theory does not always work out in practical terms, it does at least suggest a degree of self-effacing modesty on the part of the architect who formulated it that is somewhat at variance with the image of a totalitarian monster. A few years earlier Mies had designed an ideal museum for a small city [34], and here again he had tried to make the architecture 'almost nothing' and the paintings and sculpture (for which the museum would be built) everything. His beautiful drawings and collages for this project show a large, glass-enclosed space, lightly subdivided by free-standing walls and screens against which to hang paintings or place sculpture. Indeed, Mies's incredible modesty was never better expressed than in the collages he prepared for this project: for in these the only elements visible at first are the photographic reproductions of important paintings and pieces of sculpture; one must actually search with a magnifying glass for any evidence of the architecture that is supposed to enclose these works of art, for the only indication of any building whatsoever is a series of fine lines suggesting a few slender columns and the paving pattern of the floor. How different from Wright's Guggenheim Museum, whose powerful, plastic forms overwhelm all but the most self-assertive works of art!

34. Project for a museum for a small city, 1942. This collage shows Picasso's 'Guernica' among other works of art displayed. Since the museum was designed to serve the paintings displayed (rather than vice versa, as in Wright's Guggenheim Museum), there is an almost complete anonymity of architectural expression. (Courtesy, Mies van der Rohe)

Nor was the *House Beautiful* episode very edifying for Dr Farnsworth. She let herself be persuaded to grant an interview to the magazine, and her quoted remarks were not in the best of taste.

Something should be said and done about such architecture as this [she told *House Beautiful*] or there will be no future for architecture . . . I thought you could animate a predetermined, classic form like this with your own presence. I wanted to do something 'meaningful', and all I got was this glib, false sophistication.

Her principal complaints were that the house cost far too much to build ($73,000), that it was terribly impractical in many ways, and that it was expensive to maintain. Many of her criticisms would have been entirely justified if her house had been meant to be a model for 'family living'. But obviously there was no such intention. The Farnsworth house was meant to be, and succeeded in being, a clear and somewhat abstract expression of an architectural ideal – the ultimate in skin-and-bones architecture, the ultimate in 'less is more', the ultimate in objectivity and universality. And it was meant to show that even when architecture approaches nothingness, its spirit can be romantic and beautiful. The glass prism built by Mies for his friend was a mirror held up to a lovely landscape; it was not a very practical house for Levittown, say, and it was not intended to be. But it was a clear and precise statement that other, lesser architects have found very helpful indeed as a point of departure. Mies's insistence upon an all-glass skin was no arbitrary defiance of 'practicality'; it was an attempt to arrive at an absolutely clear, visual separation of structure and non-structure. All great houses by great architects tend to be somewhat impractical; many of Corbu's and Wright's house clients find that they are living in too expensive and too inefficient buildings. Yet many of these same clients would never exchange their houses for the most workable piece of mediocrity 'designed' by means of a consumer survey.

And, finally, Frank Lloyd Wright was involved in the *House Beautiful* affair as well.

The 'International Style' . . . is totalitarianism [Wright announced]. These Bauhaus architects ran from political totalitarianism in Germany to what is now made by specious promotion to seem their own totalitarianism in art here in America . . . Why do I distrust and defy such 'internationalism' as I do Communism? Because both must by their nature do this very levelling in the name of civilization . . . [The promoters of the International Style] are not a wholesome people . . .

35. General view of Crown Hall. The roof is hung from deep steel girders overhead. (Photo: Hedrich-Blessing)

Wright's fundamental disagreement with skin-and-bones architecture was nothing new, and, in many respects, was valid indeed. But his personal attack upon Mies and others was both new and unworthy of him.

Mies designed two other important 'universal' structures during the year after the Farnsworth house was completed. In 1952 he completed the plans for the Architecture and Design Building at I.I.T. [35–7], and in 1953 he submitted his proposal for a National Theatre to be built at Mannheim, in Western Germany [38].

These two structures carry the concept of a universal, entirely open, and entirely flexible space to its logical conclusion. Both buildings are framed in steel, with deep steel girders or trusses spanning the distance between outside columns. As a result, there is no need for any interior supports at all, so that the enclosed space can serve any number of different and changing functions. In both buildings the deep girders are *above* the roof plane, so that the roof ceiling (which was hung from the overhead girders) becomes a flat

slab uninterrupted by any dropped beams. All exterior walls between columns are of glass.

The Architecture and Design Building – Crown Hall – was completed in 1955, and it now houses both the School of Architecture and the Institute of Design (known as I.D.). The latter – an offspring of the Chicago version of the Bauhaus, originally started by Moholy-Nagy in the 1930s and long housed in a neo-Romanesque castle north of the Chicago Loop – was absorbed by I.I.T. in the early 1950s. Mies, who was somewhat critical of the Institute's 'undisciplined' method of operation, put the I.D. spaces into a semi-basement space below the huge studios reserved for the architecture students on the main floor. While this may seem a cruel jest, the I.D. spaces are actually well lighted by high clerestory windows all around the perimeter of the building.

37. Stair at Crown Hall. (Photo: Hedrich-Blessing)

The Mannheim Theatre remained a project. Together with a dozen other architects, Mies had been invited by the City of Mannheim to submit a proposal for its National Theatre. His design consisted of a rectangular cage of grey-tinted glass, 530 feet long, 270 feet wide, and 40 feet high, suspended between fourteen huge steel columns joined, in pairs, above the roof by seven deep steel trusses that spanned the entire 270-foot width of the building! The glass cage was held within this framework about fifteen feet above the ground level, and the entrance to the theatre was from below. Within the huge glass cage, there was room for two separate theatres, complete with workshops, dressing-rooms, and other services.

Although Mies's proposal attracted the greatest attention and was highly praised as an original contribution to architecture, the City of Mannheim chose another design, which has since been built. The completed theatre owes a good deal to Mies, but it has none of the verve and daring of his own proposal.

In developing the Mannheim project, Mies again made the point that only a universal space, free of all interior columns and infinitely flexible in interior arrangement, could hope to satisfy all the functional needs that might arise in the course of the life of the building. This notion of universality has one serious drawback, demonstrated both in the Farnsworth house and in the I.I.T building: because the large, universal space is so dramatic and exciting, Mies (and most other architects) are tempted to leave the space as undivided as possible, never carrying partitions within all the way up to the ceiling plane if this can be avoided. The result is that many of these universal spaces do not offer very satisfactory answers to problems of acoustics and controlled lighting. At Crown Hall, for example, where all partitions separating studios stop short of the ceiling plane, there are disturbing squeaks every time a student moves his stool an inch this way or that, and the constant squeaks are 'universally' audible. And in the Mannheim Theatre project it might well have been necessary to enclose the universal space with heavy curtains to keep out disturbing natural light.

All these minor and major irritations could easily be avoided if Mies were a little less stubborn. Unfortunately, he became so annoyed with some of his critics, who believed that you could substitute 'climate control' for architecture, that he adamantly refused for many years to try to do anything about these mundane problems of practical living. Still, some of his most recent work suggests that he

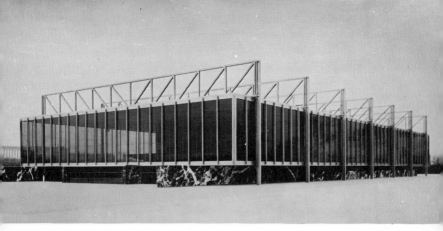

38. Mannheim Theatre project, 1953. Huge steel trusses span the entire width of the building and hold the roof plane. Small human figure at left suggests scale of the building. (Photo: Hedrich-Blessing)

has at last decided to face up to the more prosaic facts of life, and that he is perfectly capable of coping with them. He does not particularly like to admit this, saying, when asked about such things as air-conditioning or garbage collection, that 'this is not my *métier*'; but he and his associates have found that there is really no good reason why a beautiful building cannot work efficiently as well. In 1950 Mies made one of his rare speeches at I.I.T. and said, among other things, that 'some people are convinced that architecture will be outmoded and replaced by technology'. This was a sly 'dig' at the Institute of Design. 'Such a conviction is not based on clear thinking,' Mies continued. 'The opposite happens: wherever technology reaches its real fulfilment, it transcends into architecture. It is true that architecture depends on facts, but its real field of activity is in the realm of significance.' Only thirty years earlier most avant-gardists of Mies's generation were convinced that anything that expressed function and technological advance was, *ipso facto*, beautiful. Mies, of course, had never believed such nonsense; but he had found it necessary to expose the fallacy that 'functionalism must equal beauty' on more than one occasion. He may, perhaps, be forgiven if the fallacy of this equation finally persuaded him – for a short while, at least – that functionalism was, in fact, the *enemy* of beauty.

Sometime in 1946, while Mies was still Director of Architecture at
I.I.T., he met a young man, a former philosophy student, called
Herbert Greenwald, who had, by a series of accidents, become a
real-estate investor and builder just before the outbreak of the
Second World War. Greenwald was only twenty-nine years old
when he met Mies, but the two got along well from the start. The
chief reason was that Greenwald was not a builder primarily for
profit, but, rather, an idealist interested in 'leaving his stamp on the
scene', as Mies put it, by means of creating the finest architecture
possible within the framework of modern technology and modern
economics. Another reason was that both liked to talk about
philosophy.

Two years after Mies and Greenwald met, the first Mies-designed
Greenwald building, the Promontory Apartments, rose on Chicago's
Lakeshore Drive. It was a concrete-framed structure, whose bays
were filled in with brick and glass. The principal innovation – apart
from the austere simplicity of the façades – was the way in which
Mies handled the column expression: as columns obviously carry
smaller loads at the top floors than they do at street level, Mies
stepped back his columns at various levels on the principal façaαes
to make the columns progressively smaller as they rose up to the
roof-line. The result was a subtle elongation of the façade similar to
that achieved by stepped-back buttresses on medieval structures.
Several years later, when Mies designed and built the faculty apartment blocks that today adjoin the I.I.T. campus, he used the same
stepped-back concrete frame to give his buildings an exaggerated
vertical perspective – a rather subtle variation on the plain, rectangular 'slab' buildings then, and now, in vogue.

*39. Apartment houses at 860 Lakeshore Drive, Chicago, 1951. The sides of the tower
receding from view seem opaque because of the overlap of deep vertical rails that rise to th
full height of the façades. (Photo: Ezra Stoller)*

When the Promontory Apartments demonstrated the success of Mies's simplicity and logic combined with Greenwald's practical idealism, the two proceeded to bigger and more exciting things. In 1950, on another site on the shores of Lake Michigan, two steel-and-glass towers designed by Mies rose to demonstrate in full scale and for the first time what Mies tried to say in his glass-tower sketches of thirty years before. The apartments at 860 Lakeshore Drive – which soon became known, among architects all over the world, simply as '860' – were the strongest, purest, and most deceptively simple statement of his ideas which Mies had ever made.

The two towers at '860' are rectangular in plan and twenty-six storeys high [39]. They are spaced a short distance apart and set at right angles to one another, so that each apartment gets the best possible view of Lake Michigan. The buildings are all steel and glass; columns and beams are covered in black steel plate, and vertical I-beam sections of black steel spaced about five feet apart are welded to the exterior. These I-beam rails run the full height of the building, and floor-to-ceiling panels of glass framed in natural aluminium are set between the rails. There are four apartments to each floor in one building, eight in the other. At ground-floor level the two towers are connected by a black steel canopy [40].

The structural expression Mies chose for '860' is unusual and original in the extreme. While the buildings are steel-framed, the Chicago building code required the steel to be fireproofed with two inches of concrete all around. If Mies had just left his buildings as a 'bare' fireproofed structure, he would have had two vertical cages of concrete filled in with glass. The result would have been an indeterminate building, neither vertical nor horizontal, for the column and beam pattern would have created a series of *horizontal* rectangles twenty-one feet wide and about nine feet high, while the complete façade itself would have been decidedly *vertical*.

To avoid this visual conflict, Mies finished all his concrete-covered columns and beams with black steel plate, and then welded on to this black steel plate a pattern of slim, vertical I-beam rails eight inches deep, which soar from the second-floor line of the building in a pattern of closely spaced vertical strips all the way up to the roof-line 250 feet above. These slim rails give the façades a fluted appearance that suggests the vertical fluting found in the late Gothic cathedrals. They make the '860' towers the most vertical-looking skyscrapers built up to that time.

40. *Connecting canopy between apartment towers at 860 Lakeshore Drive.*
(Photo: Hedrich-Blessing)

Needless to say, the functionalists were horrified: here Mies was using steel (a structural material) as applied ornament! It was inexcusable! Mies, who takes great delight in making the functionalists squirm, explained his heresy with engaging frankness and wit. 'Now, first I am going to tell you the *real* reason for those mullions,' he told an interviewer, 'and then I am going to tell you a good reason by itself.' Where the I-beams formed window separations, he explained, they made perfectly good sense. You had to have a metal rail to separate the windows from one another, and you might as well make the mullions deep and narrow instead of wide and flat. But what about then taking those same deep and narrow I-beams and welding them on to the black steel that covered the concrete, which, in turn, covered the *real* column? Wasn't that a pretty far-fetched way to 'express' a structural frame?

It was very important to preserve and extend the rhythm which the mullions set up on the rest of the building [Mies said, coming back to the *real* reason]. We looked at it on the model without the steel I-beams attached to the corner columns and *it did not look right*. That is the *real* reason. Now, the other reason is that the steel I-beams were needed to stiffen the plates which cover the columns so these plates would not ripple, and also we needed the I-beams for strength when the sections were hoisted into place. Now, of course, that's a very *good* reason – but the other one is the *real* reason!

The *real* reason turned out to be enormously persuasive. One of the results of having a pattern of deep, vertical I-beams running up and down on all four sides of the building is that it makes the rectangular towers infinitely more plastic than a flat façade. For when you see the towers head on, one façade on each tower appears to be all glass – a huge mirror reflecting the sky and the clouds, as well as one another. But the other façade that recedes from the onlooker appears completely opaque and solid. As one walks around the buildings, the façades that were formerly opaque become open and glassy. This extraordinary play of transparency and opacity – all within the eight-inch depth of the façades – is much more subtle than Corbu's treatment of a slab like the Swiss Pavilion in Paris, where he simply made both end-walls of solid masonry to achieve the same effect, and thereby sacrificed possible window openings on two sides of his building.

In practical terms, the *real* reason turned out to be unexpectedly valid also. Mies had used the steel-plate covers on columns and beams as forms into which he poured the required concrete fire-proofing. In most buildings prior to '860' such forms were built of wood and had to be stripped off after the concrete had been poured into the wooden mould and had hardened around the steel frame. After that, the raw concrete would, generally, have to be finished with some facing material to make it look less crude. By making his forms of steel plate and welding the I-beam stiffeners to the steel plate before it was hoisted up into place, Mies killed two birds with one stone: he got his formwork into which to pour the concrete, and he could leave the formwork in place and let it be the finished surface of his structure. Several years later, when I. M. Pei, the young Chinese-born architect, designed his handsome Mile High Center office building in Denver, Colorado, he found that it was very difficult indeed to get away from Mies's rationale of this sort of cage building. Indeed, he deliberately discarded some of Mies's details for '860' – although he recognized that they made great practical sense – because he did not want to be guilty of plagiarism. In short, the 'applied decoration' in steel on top of the true structural frame at '860' turned out to be a remarkably sensible solution.

In several other respects, too, '860' represented the clarification of Mies's views. Although the building codes forced him to conceal his real structural cage, he felt that the verticality of the structure should

41. Part of the Chicago skyline, photographed from Lake Michigan in 1959. At the centre are four glass apartment towers built by Mies: the two towers at 860 Lakeshore Drive on the left, and the later, blacker towers on Lakeshore Drive, on the right. Other new buildings nearby show Mies van der Rohe's strong influence. (Photo: Hedrich-Blessing)

be clearly expressed on the façades, as it was, in a sense, the 'significance' of the skyscraper. He was giving structure a *poetic* voice in his building, because prose (i.e., the building codes) did not permit his structural cage to declare itself. The '860' buildings have often been denounced as 'cold' or 'inhuman'. They are neither. They are flights of fancy and of romance, crystal shafts rising out of a huge lake. Mies had learned the effectiveness of *pilotis* from Corbu, and so these twin towers were raised on stilts above the ground. Twenty-six storeys farther up, this separation of building from earth becomes an exhilarating experience analogous only to flight itself. For here, looking out through the glass walls of '860', one feels suspended half-way between the shimmering lake and the sky, floating in a calm and dreamlike world far removed from the chaos of the city. No building by Wright has ever conveyed more of a sense of romance.

In the apartments themselves Mies once again put to a test his theory of universality. Because of the wide and regular spacing of columns, each apartment plan is quite flexible. When *Life* published a story on Mies several years ago, the editors included some remarkable photographs showing several floors of apartments at '860' lit up at night. Each apartment, it turned out, was decorated in an entirely different manner: some owners had brought in antiques and applied classical mouldings to all walls and doors; others had bought Mies-designed chairs and tables. Although the building presents a uniform and orderly pattern to the outside world – because, according to Mies, an orderly building can be a powerful force for greater order in the world around it – each apartment seemed to offer a maximum degree of freedom of self-expression to those who live inside it.

Mies, incidentally, was never one of them. He did have an apartment reserved for him, and the move into '860' would not have been very troublesome, as his old apartment was located only a block or two away. But Mies is a man of slow motion; he hates travel, and he hates dislocation. He finally decided to stay where he was, although Greenwald and many other friends urged him to join them in the beautiful new buildings.

'860' was an economic as well as aesthetic success, and Greenwald was soon commissioning Mies to build more of the same, both in

101

Chicago and elsewhere. Before long, Mies completed two towers, clad in aluminium and glass, farther up along Chicago's North Shore. Shortly afterwards he added two more steel-and-glass towers to the ones at '860', so that Chicago now has an impressive stretch of uninterrupted Mies-designed lake front [41]. Greenwald was also developing projects in Detroit, Brooklyn, Manhattan's Battery Park, and Newark, New Jersey [42 and 43]. Before long, Mies was spending almost two-thirds of his working time on urban redevelopment projects financed by Herbert Greenwald.

Then, one day in 1959, Mies and an assistant were getting into a plane in Havana, Cuba, where Mies was about to start on a concrete-and-glass office building for the Bacardi Company. His eye caught a newspaper headline that said that a plane had crashed into New York's East River. 'That's incredible – how can anyone crash into that little stream?' Mies said to his assistant. Upon landing in New York a few hours later, Miles read the details. Among those killed in the East River crash was his friend, Herb Greenwald, forty-two years old.

43. Lafayette Park, Detroit, 1960. A development consisting of a tall apartment tower and two-storey terrace houses, all arranged in a pattern of interlocking squares. (Photo: George Cserna)

THIRTEEN

One day in the summer of 1954, while Mies was working on the Architecture Building for I.I.T., a young American woman living in Paris opened the New York papers and saw there a rendering of a tall office building her father was proposing to build on Park Avenue. The lady's name was Mrs Phyllis Bronfman Lambert, and her father was Samuel Bronfman, President of Joseph E. Seagram & Sons, the distillers. Mrs Lambert, who had taken several advanced college courses in architecture and related arts, thought that the proposed Seagram Building pictured in the New York papers looked more like a design for a 'gift decanter' than a distinguished work of architecture, and flew back to New York to have a heart-to-heart talk with her father. The outcome of this talk was that her father released his architects and authorized her to search for the best possible man to design the most distinguished skyscraper that art and technology could produce, and money could buy.

Through a friend at the Museum of Modern Art, Phyllis Lambert met Philip Johnson, who was then the Director of the Museum's Department of Architecture, and, under Johnson's guidance, went to see every major architect in the U.S. and looked at every important building put up by leading architects, young or old. She also talked to critics, magazine editors – anyone of any standing in the world of American architecture.

It has been said that Frank Lloyd Wright was the greatest architect of the nineteenth century [Mrs Lambert wrote to a friend during those months of exploration]. To me [his] Johnson Wax [building] is a complete statement of 'Manifest Destiny', the embodiment of all the philosophy of that period in America. It has a force and vitality that is almost cyclonic. It's crazy as hell and as wonderful as it is crazy . . . [But] his is not the statement that is needed now.

As for Corbu, whom she considered at length, she wrote that he has not built a building in this country . . . Would he be a great and good

44. Seagram Building, New York City, 1958. Designed in association with Philip C. Johnson. The façade is of bronze and grey-tinted glass. (Photo: Ezra Stoller)

influence here? I am afraid not ... One is fascinated by his spaces, his sculptural forms, but are not people likely to be blinded by these and skip over the surface only?

Whether or not one agrees with her judgements – especially her judgement of Corbu – it is obvious that she took her assignment very seriously and went through a long period of soul-searching. Finally, through Johnson, she met Mies and saw '860'. She had heard everyone talk about Mies long before she met him.

The younger men, the second generation, are talking in terms of Mies – or denying him [she had written]. They talk of new forms – articulating the skin or facades to get a play of light and shadow. But Mies has said: 'Form is not the aim of our work, but only the result.' ... He has articulated the skin [of his buildings], at the same time creating a play of depth and shadow by the use of the basic structural steel member, the I-beam. This ingenious and deceptively simple solution is comparable to the use of the Greek orders ... It is not a capricious solution; it is the essence of the problem of modern architecture that Mies had stated in 1922: 'We should develop the new forms from the very nature of the new problems.'

So Mies was selected to design the new Seagram Building, and he, in turn, asked Philip Johnson (who was registered as an architect in New York State) to associate with him on the project. Three and a half years later, in the summer of 1958, the thirty-eight-storey bronze-and grey-glass tower on Park Avenue was formally opened [44–7]. By almost any standards the building was a superlative success. Lewis Mumford, the advocate of open spaces and of more humanism in the city, wrote delightedly that the open plaza in front of the elegant tower, which represented a wonderfully conspicious 'waste' of some fifty per cent of the site, set an important example for others to emulate. As for the bronze finish on the building, Mumford admired its 'warmth' and pointed out that Mies could no longer be considered a 'cold' architect in the light of this performance. Henry-Russell Hitchcock said that he had never seen 'more of less'. And the British architect Peter Smithson – a leader of the so-called New Brutalist cult in England – admired the Seagram Building's elegance and *lack* of brutality. 'Everything else [in Manhattan] now looks like a jumped-up supermart,' he said.

Indeed, the most remarkable effect of Seagram's triumph was what the building did to some of the fine work around it: diagonally across Park Avenue stands the handsome Lever House, based originally upon Mies's glass towers of the early twenties, but now looking a little too slick, a little too much like a Cadillac next to Seagram's Rolls-Royce nobility. Curiously enough, it was only the sixty-year-old Italianate Racquet Club designed by classicists McKim, Mead & White, directly across from Seagram on Park Avenue, that could look the new bronze tower straight in the eye without flinching.

This, of course, was no accident. For at Seagram Mies built an essentially classical building – symmetrical, formal, raised on a granite-paved plaza bordered by a marble parapet and inlaid with two rectangular pools. Superficially, Seagram is quite similar to *one* of the '860' towers; but the point, at '860', is that there were first *two* towers and later four, so that the composition on Lakeshore Drive was always asymmetrical and dynamic, whereas the composition of the Seagram tower is axial, monumental, noble, and in repose. How much of this was due to Johnson – whose own glass house is so much more 'traditional' and 'European' than Mies's Farnsworth house – is hard to say. Of course, all the basic ideas originated with Mies. Like '860', the Seagram tower is raised on stilts, and the lobby is a volume enclosed in glass, deeply recessed behind the main façades of the tower. As a result, the ground floor of the building is surrounded by magnificent arcades, twenty-eight feet high. Above these arcades the tower soars upward to its full height of 520 uninterrupted feet, the vertical stressed by the same sort of applied I-beam mullions that give '860' its rhythm (though at Seagram the I-beam extrusions are of bronze). There is added drama in the verticality of Seagram, for the building was set back from the avenue almost a hundred feet, so that pedestrians can really see the full height of this tower. By contrast, other Manhattan buildings, which tend to crowd the sidewalks, look puny because no pedestrian can really see them in their full height. Mies feels that a building deserves to be walked up to, not just driven into: for nobody dashing into an entrance lobby from an automobile portico will ever experience the full drama of a skyscraper. Actually, the Seagram Building does have canopied side entrances, for use on rainy days, as well as a large, underground drive-in garage.

Inside the glass lobby the symmetry is carried though in the

45. *Seagram Plaza as seen from the roof of the Racquet Club on the opposite side of Park Avenue. Venetian blinds for the building were designed to assume only three positions: all the way up, all the way down, or at half-mast.* (*Photo: George Cserna*)

46. *Seagram lobby, looking out over the plaza. The Racquet Club by McKim, Mead & White is at right. (Photo: George Cserna)*

arrangement of travertine-sheathed lift shafts. At night these blocks of travertine are washed in light from coves recessed in the ceiling. Indeed, the entire building was designed with a view to night lighting: all office spaces around the perimeter have luminous ceilings that give a uniform effect to the bronze cage when the building is lit up after dark.

Rarely has a building been designed with such painstaking care all the way through. No doorknob, no lavatory or tap, no sign, no mail chute was left to accident. All were carefully designed to make the building a unified whole. Much of the interior work was done by Johnson, and he carried Mies's discipline into every single detail, however seemingly unimportant. Works of art were bought or specially commissioned for the Seagram Company's own floors, and much of Mies's own timeless furniture of the 1920s was used in those offices. The ultimate in perfection was probably reached in the design of the Seagram executives' men's room – a little retreat of travertine, white leather, stainless steel, and glass which would have pleased the Emperor Tiberius.

When the Seagram Building was ready to open, every architect of

47. Approach to the main entrance of the Seagram Building. Since the structure was completed in 1958, its bronze façade has gradually turned the colour of an old penny. (Photo: Ezra Stoller)

note in New York attended. Only Mies was absent, for his legs were almost completely paralysed by one of his recurring attacks of arthritis. He had not been in New York very much during the months when the finishing touches were applied to the building, for apart from being hindered in his travels by his sickness, he was annoyed by a gratuitous slap administered to him by the authorities in charge of licensing architects in New York State. These gentlemen had noted that he was licensed in Illinois only, and had requested him to go through the formalities of New York State registration before continuing with his work on Seagram. When Mies tried to do so, it was discovered to the horror of New York's bureaucrats that he had never completed his high-school examination! When it was suggested to him that he might take a high-school examination, Mies packed up and returned to Chicago in disgust. Johnson later managed to straighten things out, and Mies may now practice architecture in New York State without risking a prison sentence!

Seagram was an expensive building, possibly the most expensive skyscraper, per square foot, ever built up to that time. Yet it seemed to repay much of its cost in terms of good public relations and other intangibles, and the paved plaza in front of the building gave it such nobility and 'prestige' that numerous banks offered large sums to the Seagram Company for the right to build branch offices on the plaza, not realizing, apparently, that the desecration of the plaza would rob the site of the very nobility the prestige-hungry bankers were willing to purchase at such high cost!

In some respects, Seagram represented the ultimate development of Mies's glass towers – the final perfection of the more or less smooth glass-and-metal curtain wall. Compared to the flat and crude curtain walls all around it in Manhattan, Seagram had the distinction of a brooch by Cartier over a piece of cheap 'costume jewellery'. Yet, to most architects in America, it raised one obvious question: 'Where do we go from here?' For Mies this question did not exist; so long as logic (i.e., existing technology) led unerringly to the rectangular steel cage, so long as the I-beam was the pilaster of our century and, hence, symbolized 'structure' – so long did Truth and Beauty lie along a straight and narrow road lined by buildings like '860' and Seagram.

Yet there were many others whose convictions about architecture, truth, and beauty were less firm and rigid; and these more flexible men started to find themselves subjected to pressures from unexpected quarters – pressures intended to force them to produce 'something new' regardless of whether the novelty was in any way valid. The forces that demand novelty for novelty's sake – or, rather, novelty for advertising's sake – are familiar enough in business: indeed, the U.S. economy would cease to function if it were not for the stylists who produce new models of this dress or that automobile every six months or every year, and thus force the average consumer to buy the new model or face social ostracism. During the years of plenty in America, the 1950s in particular, these pressures to produce 'something new' began to be applied to artists as well, and many of the weaker ones became victims. A talented composer presented a work of music consisting of several minutes of dead silence. (It was, quite possibly, his best work; but was it art?) A talented painter began to exhibit canvases showing nothing (he was immediately hailed by the taste makers as a bright new star on the artistic firmament). And so forth. The undeniable fact was that the taste makers, like the promoters of streamlined electric toasters and automobiles with fish tails, had found it necessary to push for novelty or face professional ruin. Magazines did not want to publish anything that looked the same', so they published buildings that looked like fish or turtles; museum directors had to keep the trustees and the public amused, so they exhibited buildings that looked like chickens or eggs. The pressure was on full blast: unless an architect was willing to face *critical* ostracism, he had to jump on the hucksters' bandwagon.

To Mies all this was not only nonsense, it was worse than that – heresy and dishonesty. 'I ask myself,' he said speaking of a particularly convoluted building that had just made the front page of a magazine, 'what this thing would look like on Michigan Avenue. *That* is the problem of our epoch! They [the " news makers "] say they are bored with my objectivity. Well, I am bored with their subjectivity!' It was not that Mies was trying to perpetuate an old-fashioned technology simply in order to perpetuate his own form of expression. (Indeed, in 1946, when he had first become acquainted with the structural properties of reinforced plastics, Mies designed a number of compound-curved chairs very similar in form to conch shells. This was long before most architects began to play the 'shell game', and it made obvious sense in terms of *chair* technology and *chair* function.) But everyone familiar with the problems of American building today and in the foreseeable future knows that the rectangular frame of steel or concrete, within certain minor variations of detail, is the only logical kind of structure for most buildings in economic and technical terms. Undoubtedly this harsh fact of life imposes upon American architects a discipline – even a straitjacket – which many of them are tempted to throw off. Every issue of every architectural magazine shows one or two buildings that torture structure – buildings that reflect, with terrifying clarity, the desperate and presently fruitless struggles of certain architects to break through the limitations imposed by technology. These tortured buildings are the agonies of those who lack the stern faith of Mies – the faith that rests upon St Augustine's 'Beauty is the splendour of Truth'. Mies, also, needs an outlet for creativity, and he finds it in the perfection of details. (For his Bacardi building in Cuba, Mies made more than a hundred detailed studies of the profile for the eight concrete columns that hold up the roof.) But novelty for its own sake? That, to Mies, disqualifies a man from being an architect. 'I don't want to be interesting,' Mies told an interviewer. 'I want to be good!'

In the architectural schools of the United States, Europe, and the Far East, Mies today reigns supreme. The unfaltering logic of his steel cage filled with glass or brick, the convincing strength of his concept of universality to serve a world of rapidly changing needs and functions, and the fact, finally, that Mies's work (as Philip Johnson has said) seems so easy to copy – these have made Miesian architecture the simplest and most flexible vocabulary available to today's architectural students. And his influence is by no means confined to the schools: in England, Germany, Japan – as well as throughout the United States – architects originally trained in a freer idiom have today accepted Mies's discipline, because they have found it the most logical way of applying the available technology to modern problems. Only in the concrete-building countries – France, Italy, the South American countries, etc. – is Mies's rectangular discipline challenged by the plasticity of Le Corbusier.

This does not mean that Mies's followers have invariably succeeded in translating Miesian technology into architecture. Much of today's Miesian work is little more than a re-use, for eminently practical reasons, of Mies's details and his basic principles of planning. The refinement of proportion, the perfection of workmanship – these are often lacking. For Mies has only provided a vocabulary; most use it to write prose; only a few can write poetry. Still, a coherent prose-vocabulary is one of the most urgent needs of architecture today – just as it was when the beautiful New England towns were first constructed from carpenters' 'pattern-books'.

By comparison with Corbu, Gropius, and Wright, Mies has dedicated himself to a very limited area of endeavour: where the other three treated the whole world and all its problems as part of their concern, Mies seems to have drawn a tight circle in the sand and said: 'Only these things within this circle are the concerns of architecture.' Outside this tight circle, Mies has placed problems of political and physical planning on a large scale, problems of painting and sculpture,

48. Administration building for the Bacardi Company, Santiago, Cuba, 1958. The coffered concrete roof is supported on eight, cross-shaped concrete columns. The glass pavilion on the pedestal contains a large office space; the pedestal itself holds subsidiary offices and storage spaces. (Photo: Hedrich-Blessing)

problems of theoretical speculation. Indeed, he has even left out some problems of function which are rightly considered a part of the architect's area of activity, and he has left them out at his own peril. To him, architecture has always been a single, simple progression, from material through technology to significant form and art.

His apparent narrowness when compared to far-ranging men like Gropius, Corbu, and Wright has had several distinct advantages: for one thing, Mies became a master of the limited field he had outlined for himself, whereas the others became generalizers of ideas, rather than specialists in any given area. No one in our time has built with as much attention to detail as Mies; both Corbu and Wright have often ignored the details of building – Mies, never. For another, Mies has never deviated from the *possible*. Others in search of new forms or symbols or techniques to alleviate the boredom within themselves have often strayed all over the place; Mies, who once told his students that 'education must lead us . . . from chance and arbitrariness to rational clarity and intellectual order', has never been tempted to wander into the Disneyland of modern architecture. To him, there are no laws that dictate forms in architecture; but there *are* laws that demand responsibility, clarity, and intellectual order. He has often been criticized for 'working with blinkers on'. To this Mies answers that

if it were necessary to make curves, I would make curves. [But] as long as we have this same economic and scientific structure, steel will be the essence of our cities. Our buildings need not look alike. After all, there are about 10,000 species of seashells. They don't look alike, but they have the same principle. The trouble is that most architects try to invent something every time. *The real thing is a very slow unfolding of form. We should refine what is known. And when a new problem comes along, then we'll know how to solve it.*

A new problem came along late in 1958, when Mies was asked to design the Bacardi office building in Santiago, Cuba. The problem was concrete, and Mies solved it with tremendous verve: on a classic pedestal similar to that which supported the Barcelona Pavilion, Mies proposed to place a structure of eight cross-shaped, tapered concrete columns to carry a concrete roof plane some 180 feet square [48 and 49]. This roof was to have been a five-foot-deep concrete egg crate, and its column supports were to occur approximately fifty feet in from each of the four corners, so that the corners themselves would be deeply cantilevered from the supports. The roof would thus seem to float almost twenty-five feet above the paved pedestal. The grey-tinted glass walls of the great office space were recessed twenty feet from the face of the roof plane so that the interior would be shaded most of the time. As Bacardi's owners wanted a single large room in which to conduct their operations, Mies divided the great space only by three low, free-standing partitions. The pedestal on which the building stands is high enough so that many of the service rooms can be accommodated below the glass room.

'The trouble as well as the advantage of concrete is that you can do anything with it,' Philip Johnson once said. 'You can't rely on structural discipline as a guide.' Almost anyone except Mies would have run riot with his first all-concrete building; indeed, others who profess to be influenced by Mies have abandoned all architectural restraint when they first encountered this flexible material. But Bacardi, though unmistakably a design in reconstructed stone – almost a modern version of the Parthenon set on its own formal Acropolis – remains an intensely moral building: serene, clear, unaffected, pure, and utterly self-assured. It might have done for modern *concrete* architecture what the Farnsworth house did for modern *steel* architecture – that is, bring its practitioners back to their senses. Unfortunately the project was abandoned after the Castro revolution.

114

49. Detail of typical column for the Bacardi building. The tapered concrete columns are topped with a stainless steel 'hinge' on which the roof is supported. (Courtesy, Mies van der Rohe)

By the middle of 1959 Mies was very busy indeed. He had just completed a museum in Houston, Texas, and, though he had to attend its opening in a wheelchair, his arthritis had let up considerably since then and he was almost as spry as in the old days. The Bacardi Company had commissioned him to build another structure in Mexico City [50 and 51]; the U.S. State Department had asked him to design the new Consulate General in São Paulo, Brazil; and several of Herb Greenwald's projects would probably go ahead, despite Greenwald's death. Like all the other 'Grand Old Men' of modern architecture, Mies was beginning to collect honours right and left. In the summer of 1959 he went to London to receive the Royal Gold

50. *Bacardi Building, Mexico City, 1961. This is the narrow end view of the dark grey steel and glass structure. The ground floor contains only an entrance lobby and arcades; all offices are upstairs. (Photo: Richard Davis)*

51. *Two-storey-high entrance hall of the Bacardi Building in Mexico City. Office spaces are on the mezzanine level. (Photo: Richard Davis)*

Medal for Architecture from Queen Elizabeth II. After that, there was a medal or two to pick up in his native Germany, where his home town of Aachen also honoured him by naming a street after him. And in 1960 the American Institute of Architects awarded him *its* Gold Medal as well. Wherever he went, there were enthusiastic and curious admirers. For Mies, the man who had swept modern architecture cleaner than anyone else, was virtually unknown as a person. And after the embarrassment of all the publicity was over, Mies returned to his quiet and uncluttered apartment in Chicago with a sigh of relief.

Mies would probably deny any direct influence upon his work on the part of the Catholic Church. 'The whole trend of our time is toward the secular,' he wrote in 1924. 'We shall build no cathedrals . . . Ours is not an age of pathos; we do not respect flights of the spirit as much as we value reason and realism.' And, a year earlier: 'Architecture is the will of an epoch translated into space – living, changing, new.' *The will of an epoch* – and Mies has never considered himself to be more than an instrument of that will, just as the great architects of the past were instruments of the will of their epoch. 'Greek temples, Roman basilicas and medieval cathedrals are significant to us as creations of a whole epoch rather than as works of individual architects. Who asks for the names of these builders?' Ludwig Mies van der Rohe, perhaps the most self-effacing architect of *his* epoch, the only architect modest enough to try to create an *anonymous* architecture to serve *all* of humanity – his name will be remembered when others are long forgotten.

FURTHER READING

The books that one can read about Mies van der Rohe are few, but fortunately they are good; the most important was written by his most devoted follower: *Mies van der Rohe* by Philip Johnson (Museum of Modern Art, New York, 2nd edition, 1953).

Well illustrated with excellent drawings, the work of an old associate of Mies is: *Mies van der Rohe* by Ludwig Hilbersheimer (Paul Theobald, Chicago, 1956). And there is a compact monograph in the Masters of World Architecture series: *Ludwig Mies van der Rohe* by Arthur Drexler (George Braziller Inc., New York, 1961).

Two special issues of magazines worth seeking out are: *Architectural Design,* March 1961, a special issue on Mies, edited by Peter Carter, one of his assistants; and *Architectural Review,* May 1957, *Machine-Made America,* a special issue which gives a panoramic survey of U.S. architecture at the moment of Mies's greatest influence.

INDEX

Italic numbers refer to illustrations

Some other Pelicans on architecture are described on the following pages

AN OUTLINE OF EUROPEAN
ARCHITECTURE

NIKOLAUS PEVSNER

A109

This is a history of Western architecture as an expression of Western
civilization, described in its growth from the ninth to the twentieth
century. It tells the story of architecture through the medium of its outstanding expressions in actual building. The method adopted is to discuss
a few representative buildings of each period and country in some detail
and to avoid dull cataloguing. The aim of the book is to make readers
appreciate architectural values. It is written for reading, not merely for
reference, and it makes interesting reading indeed in its concentration and
its combination of warmth and scholarship.

This famous book is now available in a seventh edition which has been
considerably revised and extended. Increased in format, the book now
contains over 300 excellent illustrations.

Professor Pevsner is head of the Department of the History of Art,
Birkbeck College, University of London. He edits the Pelican History of
Art and Architecture.

ALSO BY PETER BLAKE

LE CORBUSIER

A605

In the battle for hones[...]
who has been called[...]
unique role. Larg[...]
forced concrete, [...]
almost the normal.

In this well-illustrated stu[...]
distinguished American archite[...]
ideas almost as much in print and[...]
examples of the chapel at Ronchamp, th[...]
or the planned city of Chandigarh. He intro[...]
provocative personality who, though influenced b[...]
Art Nouveau, Machine Art, and Cubism, has never [...]
from the highroad of Mediterranean architecture.

'Should afford the lay reader a sight of Corb as he is seen by architec[...]
To read it is not only to understand better a master architect, it is t[...]
understand better all architects' – *New Statesman*

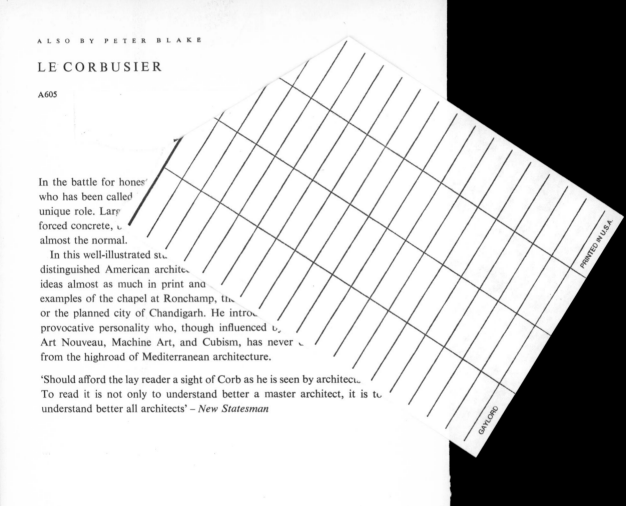